MW01506207

P k

THE ART OF RELATIONSHIP

"The wisdom of THEO, channeled by my dear friend Sheila Gillette, in this groundbreaking book is both timeless and incredibly timely. Sheila and Marcus guide you into an immersive journey of self-discovery, leading you into an expanded experience of spiritual awareness and emotional mastery. As you discover the magic of unconditional love for yourself, every relationship in our life will transform. Whatever your current relationship aspirations or challenges may be you will find the answers here to move confidently towards a life of peace, clarity and love. As a teacher for over 40 years exploring the spiritual side of relationships, I found this to be one of the most compelling books ever written on this topic."

> —Mary Morrissey, founder, Brave Thinking Institute

"Everyone wants phenomenal and exciting relationships. Our friends, Sheila and Marcus Gillette share the angelic wisdom of THEO (channeled by Sheila) that takes you into your inner-knower and the secret place of the most high—so you can create extraordinary and magnificent relationships—that will make you happier, healthier, wealthier, and living with evermore insight and wisdom. Read, relish, and enjoy their brilliance."

> —Mark Victor Hansen, co-creator of *Chicken Soup for the Soul* and the *ASK!* book series having sold over 500,000,000 books

"This is the best book you will ever read on relationships! The wisdom of Theo is brought forth from the Angelic Realm to provide humanity with new insights as we connect with one another. Thank you, Sheila and Marcus Gillette, for sharing *The Art of Relationship* with humanity!"

> —Nancy Yearout, host of High Road to Humanity

PRAISE FOR
THEO, Sheila, and Marcus

"THEO's wisdom is direct, clear, and uplifting. Anyone who takes these teachings to heart will advance spiritually and enjoy deeper peace and enriched relationships with Spirit, self, and others. I am grateful that this voice of higher truth is touching many people through the dedicated service of Sheila and Marcus."

—Alan Cohen, best-selling author of *I Had it All the Time*

"As the words flowed from Sheila/THEO, I felt them penetrate to the core of my being. A feeling of love flowed to me and through me like nothing I had ever felt before."

—Esther Hicks, Channel for Abraham

"It is always enlightening when you find the real deal: honest and informative information, cutting edge truth, and delivered with love and empowerment. This is Sheila Gillette, who channels THEO. I trust her, her love, and the greatness of the message that comes through her. She is, in every way, the real deal."

—Dee Wallace, actor, healer, and best-selling author

"As Executive Producer and host I'm regularly exposed to high levels of intellect and esoteric knowledge. The work of Sheila and the THEO group brings an even deeper level of truth and mature spiritual understanding that strikes me to the core of my own sense of higher truth. Theo communicates with clarity, compassion, directness, and integrity."

—Regina Meredith, producer and host Gaia TV

"THEO offers incredibly inspiring, authentic, and usable information. . . . This is VERY high vibrating material, that will take you to a new dimension within—creating new realities outside yourself."

—Jennifer McLean, host of *Healing with the Masters*

"The ability and knowledge to be rocketed to a higher plane of consciousness is truly a wonderful gift that THEO has given our souls."

—Dr. Howard Peiper, best-selling author of *The Secrets of Staying Young*

PRAISE FOR
THE 5TH DIMENSION: CHANNELS TO A NEW REALITY
BY SHEILA GILLETTE (1988 SIMON/SCHUSTER)

"Sheila Gillette is one of the foremost channels to appear recently. Ranking with such people as Ruth Montgomery and Greta Alexander, she has done much to foster interest in legitimate parapsychological research."

—Dr. Evan Harris Walker, noted physicist, originator
of the Observational Theory in Parapsychology
and author of *The Physics of Consciousness*

"Knowledge is essential for human growth. In the '5th Dimension' Sheila Gillette opens for us the knowledge of human goodness. Step-by-step, she guides us in the discovery of our own potential and the flow within the universe."

—Richard Corriere, Ph.D., author of
Life Zones: How to Win in the Game of Life

PRAISE FOR

THE SOUL TRUTH:
A GUIDE TO INNER PEACE
BY SHEILA AND MARCUS GILLETTE
(2009 TARCHER/PENGUIN)

"I am very impressed by the variety of responses and by the similarity
of answers that I would have given, especially regarding my favorite
topics, life after death and millennium prophecies. It is a terrific com-
panion for all souls on a spiritual journey."

—Dr. Elisabeth Kübler-Ross,
best-selling author of *On Death and Dying*

"I consider Sheila Gillette one of the special gifts of my life. She is a
friend, a confidant, a guiding force. The level of personal integrity
she brings to her work could not be greater, and the THEO energy
brought through her channeling is always a beautifully uplifting, and
profoundly informative experience"

—Joyce DeWitt, actress, ABC's #1 TV show *Three's Company*

THE ART OF
RELATIONSHIP

DISCOVER THE MAGIC OF
UNCONDITIONAL LOVE

SHEILA AND MARCUS GILLETTE
The Wisdom of THEO

The Art of Relationship

AskTHEO®™

Copyright © 2022 by THEO Press

All rights reserved. All content is subject to copyright and may not be reproduced
in any form without express written consent from the author. Although the author
and publisher have made every effort to ensure that the information in this book was
correct at press time, the author and publisher do not assume and hereby disclaim any
liability to any party for any loss, damage, or disruption caused by errors or omissions,
whether such errors or omissions result from negligence, accident, or any other cause.

Published by THEO Press

ISBN 978-0-9655457-5-4 (paperback)
ISBN 978-0-9655457-7-8 (hardcover)
ISBN 978-0-9655457-8-5 (ebook)

Printed in the United States of America

*For Our Parents—Ralph and Dorothy Williams, and Jere and
Alicia Gillette, we thank them for their love, support, and
inspiration in this lifetime, and their enduring impact and
guidance from their current state of unconditional love.*

WE ARE GRATEFUL you've purchased our book and hope it supports your creation of vibrant relationships. As you read it you may discover THEO is very selective in their word choices. They often speak to the importance of words and invite you to look up words that stand out to you in your "big book of words" (THEO's description of our dictionary), as well as reference THEO's glossary at the end of the book. Along with their word selection THEO also utilizes unique vibrational frequencies when speaking, through Sheila, which provides the listener an energetic alignment, or attunement.

As a way of expressing our gratitude we are pleased to provide additional audio gifts to deepen your relationship with yourself and others, as well as discover the myriad opportunities for you to be personally mentored by THEO.

Access these gifts at: **www.asktheo.com/gifts-aor**

CONTENTS

"Relationships are an art, an interactive artistic expression of the human experience. It is like a dance, is it not? With exquisite music playing as you dance with others in human life."

—THEO

CHAPTER ONE

OUR MULTI-DIMENSIONAL LOVE STORY

"It is a choice made by both, not just one, to have experiences to express their multi-dimensionality. Making an agreement for experiences in the etheric such as out-of-body experiences, and remembrances of other times. These experiences are as varied as the souls are, and their alignment to them."

—THEO

I FELT HIM before I ever saw him.

It was as if a powerful energy had come onto the patio at the Phoenician Resort. I glanced at my friends seated around the fire pit. They were laughing, talking, enjoying the setting sun on this gorgeous April evening. They didn't seem to notice anything unusual. The sky splashed iridescent pink, orange, and purple hues against the silhouette of Camelback Mountain. The city lights of Phoenix sparkled in the distance. I'd flown in from Colorado to give a talk and do private readings for clients over the next few days. As a spiritual medium and direct voice channel for the twelve archangels, collectively known as THEO, I was used to remarkable experiences. But this energy I was feeling was new to me. I thought, *Well, this is interesting. I wonder what this is all about?*

My awakening to expanded states of consciousness had begun many years earlier with the birth of my youngest child. Immediately after delivery, I had to be rushed to Intensive Care with uncontrollable bleeding. I'd developed a pulmonary embolism. Blot clots had broken loose and travelled through my heart to my lungs. I was drowning in my own blood. It felt like an elephant was sitting on my chest. Unable to move. Unable to breathe. The nurses encouraged me to rest, but I knew that if I closed my eyes, I would never open them again. The doctors prepared my family for my death. Alone in a tiny cubicle in the ICU, I pleaded with God, *I'll do anything. Please God. Give me a job!* Over and over, I begged. I had two young children at home and a newborn baby girl. I was desperate to come through this and be a mother to them.

Suddenly, something moved at the end of my bed. Brilliant golden light filled the room. When I looked up, I saw the most beautiful being. I was mesmerized by his kind face and beautiful hazel eyes. It was Jesus standing there. He smiled. And in my inner mind, I heard him say, "Remember my child. You are loved."

In that moment, it felt as if the crown of my head opened up and warm honey poured in. It seeped slowly down my body, penetrating every cell, and when it reached my lungs . . . I gasped! I was able to take in a deep breath. I knew my prayers had been answered and I would recover.

As my body healed and grew stronger, I began to experience all kinds of psychic phenomena. My miraculous healing had opened a doorway into new levels of perception. I no longer feared death. The world became more beautiful. Colors in nature more vivid. I discovered I now had enhanced abilities to connect to the non-physical realm—through automatic writing, telekinesis and one day . . . I spontaneously trance channeled. I spent many years practicing and developing these psychic gifts which led me to the work I do now— serving as the direct voice channel for the twelve archangels known collectively as THEO—the "job" I believe God had given me all those years ago.

I sipped my glass of wine on the hotel verandah. I was feeling an energy that was completely new to me. I didn't know who or what I was sensing. It surged. Drawing nearer. I turned to look. A tall, handsome man walked up to our table, smiling. It was Marcus. A jolt went through my body. I literally felt like the air had been knocked out of me. You know the songs that say, "You take my breath away." I thought those were just lyrics. I had never had anything like that happen before. It was more than just seeing an attractive man. This was so powerful. Immediately I knew there's something big going on here. His energy meeting my energy. Well, it was indescribable.

"What's your story?" Sheila asked.

I knew she would be beautiful. I'd seen her photo on the back of my well-worn copy of her book. But she was even more beautiful in person, softer more radiant. I explained what I did "By Day," meaning my 3D linear work with my consulting business serving corporate

America as opposed to my passion "By Night" which was my spirituality. I talked on and on—overjoyed to speak so freely about what mattered most to me with someone who understood.

The string of "coincidences" that led me to the patio that evening, I could never have orchestrated even if I tried. Two years earlier, I was in the grocery store when my inner voice insisted that I hand my business card to a complete stranger. "I don't know why I'm doing this but I am being guided for some reason to give you my card," I told her. I trusted that there was some purpose to be revealed later. This woman, Donna, turned out to be an old friend of Sheila's from Santa Fe. She called. We met, and she gave me a copy of Sheila's first book. *The 5th Dimension: Channels to a New Reality* details THEO's teachings about the emerging global spiritual transformation—much of which we're seeing playing out today. The book was precisely what I needed to be reading at that moment in my journey. It answered so many of my questions. I loved it. I shared it. I was quoting THEO and Sheila with friends. I was a fan. I was just happy to be meeting her. I wanted Sheila to know how much I respected her and her gift.

As far as anything deeper going on between us, I was pretty clueless.

Marcus and our friends attended the live event the following night. A few days later, he arrived at Donna's house for a private reading.

Once I was back home in Colorado, Marcus became a client. We also began to speak on the phone. I knew we had a powerful connection, but I didn't know if he was ever going to realize it.

I was definitely drawn to Sheila, but I was not looking for anything at the time. My last relationship had ended, in large part because I was opening up and frankly, it scared her. We separated because we'd discovered we were just not spiritually aligned. I was content. Peaceful in my knowing that what I was going through spiritually was extraordinary and I wasn't in a hurry to move into a relationship.

I *did* know that I loved speaking with Sheila and getting to know her better. It felt wonderful to share profound experiences and be understood. I told her all about my Vision Quest trips to visit the Havasupai—The People of the Blue Green Water—who lived at the bottom of the Grand Canyon—how unique the experience was because my friends and I had developed special relationships with the community elders. We were invited to camp on their land, away from any tourists and partake of ceremony the tribe didn't often share with outsiders. I promised Sheila, I would invite her the very next time we went.

"We're going to the Havasupai!" Marcus called to tell me

"I want to go! I want to go!" I was over the moon.

"We're leaving May 12th."

My heart dropped. I'd been booked months in advance for an event in Anchorage, Alaska. There was just no way I could cancel on them. We hung up. I'd hadn't even set the phone back in the cradle when it rang again. It was the bookstore in Anchorage calling to ask if we could postpone. "Absolutely!" I told them. The Angels were orchestrating—clearing our path. I called Marcus back right away. "I'm in!"

I flew to Phoenix and Marcus picked me up at the airport. We drove to Flagstaff where our group would gather and spend the night, so we could be up early for our long trek down to the bottom of the Grand Canyon on horseback.

At dinner, Sheila and I talked and laughed together nonstop. I knew something was going on between us. I just wasn't sure *what*. Our relationship was a soulful connection. It was all a bit surreal. I was just grateful to be hanging out. To be close to her.

Back in the hotel lobby. We kissed for the first time. I said good night and went back to my room. What followed is one of the most astonishing things that I ever experienced.

I was lying in bed, when suddenly, I was awakened out of a deep sleep. The clock read 2:15 a.m. I heard my roommate snoring. Below the ceiling, a shimmering oval of light hovered above my body—silver crystalline, luminescent. I had no fear at all, as I intuitively knew this energy to be Sheila in her light body. It descended slowly. When it reached my physical body, it merged with me. I lost consciousness.

I barely slept after saying good night to Marcus. I was buzzing with so much energy. The frequency was so high-pitched. As soon as it got light, I went outside, hoping that moving my body would get some of this out of me. I circled the hotel as fast as I could, waving my arms to discharge some of the electricity. A busload of sleepy German tourists pulled up. A man called out to me, "I want some of what you have!"

"I wish I could give it to you!" It was that overwhelming.

I awoke the next morning with my first thought being of my last moment of consciousness. *What in the world happened to me last night?* I was completely blown away, and wildly curious to know what Sheila had been up to the night before. I had never experienced anything like this, and I knew it was significant. About 6:30 a.m., I ran into her in the lobby. "I know where you were last night," I said.

"Did you get me?" she asked.

"Did you get me? Are you kidding me? "Yes. I got you alright." But I still did not really understand what had happened.

Twenty-five years later, I finally asked THEO what did happen that night. They told me, "Your perception is correct, for you are soulfully aligned, as you know. It was for you to be aware of the strength of the connectivity. You saw the light body as you spoke of it."

Sixty miles outside Seligman, AZ is a place the Havasupai call Hilltop where our guides saddled up the horses and packed up the gear, making ready for the journey to the bottom of Grand Canyon.

As we rode the dusty switchbacks down to the narrow trail, I had plenty of time to think about the mystery of Sheila projecting her soul to me the night before. It was a six-hour ride, 3,000 feet down to the Havasupai. I had enough spiritual experiences by then to know that souls do purposefully incarnate together. I wondered, *who are we together?*

We reached the heart of Havasu Canyon—a spectacular oasis surrounded by soaring red rock cliffs. Havasu creek bubbles up from a spring and flows through the canyon creating idyllic pools that swirl beneath a grove of cottonwoods. Turquoise water plunges over dramatic waterfalls. You don't have to know a thing about vibration to feel that this is a high frequency, magical spot where miracles and extraordinary things happen.

We played under the waterfalls in the terraced blue pools to cool off during the day. At night, we'd drag our lawn chairs out into an open field to look at the stars. Basically, we did whatever we could do to be off by ourselves. We were falling in love.

I soon discovered that I did have some competition for Sheila's affection. One night, under a beautiful waxing half-moon, a six-year-old girl Native American girl crawled right up onto Sheila's lap. She handed her a hand-made card with an "M" on one side and a half-moon on the other. Molina, the granddaughter of our Havasupai friend, was as enchanted with Sheila as I was. From then on, she was like her shadow.

As part of the trip, we were privileged to join in the sweat lodge ceremony—the most profound and direct connection to the spirit world for the Havasupai. As we waited our turn one afternoon, the smell of burning sage and juniper was heavy in the air. Molina and her little cousin, Darius, played in the creek bed near us.

As Marcus and I sat on the bank outside the sweat lodge, I suddenly felt myself transported to another time. The children now wore buckskin clothing as they played in the water. There were moccasins on my feet. I wore animal skins similar to theirs. I looked over at Marcus. He too, was in head-to-toe traditional Native American dress from another era. I described what I was experiencing. "Are you seeing what I'm seeing?"

I was. Simultaneously, we were in another time. It was clear to us that we had been together in another incarnation. These children had been *our* children. We were familiar with experiences of collapsing time and space, but those had always happened for us individually. This multi-dimensional vision felt "out of time." *And we were experiencing it together*. It might have lasted only seconds. It might have been hours. We had no idea. There was no time at all. This confirmed that we had been together before.

We fell in love with this place, as we fell in love with each other.

It was very late when we returned to my home in Scottsdale. Tired but happy, we went outside on the patio to stargaze. The increasing vibration of joy we felt over those next few hours is impossible to describe. We stayed out there all night until the first streaks of pink appeared in the East—becoming more and more golden with the arrival of the sun. As far as "first dates" go, our camping trip was bliss.

"So, what are we going to do on our second date?" I asked.

"I don't date," Sheila said.

I don't know where the words came from. I hadn't planned on saying them. My soul knew more than I did. I had no doubt.

"Well then, let's get married."

And so, we did.

We just knew that our souls had purposefully come together. We were grateful and delighted to have found each other again in this lifetime. And this would be the beginning of our playing, loving, and working together, sharing THEO with the world.

We trust that the following dialogues with THEO can shine a light on your path going forward.

CHAPTER TWO

THE SACRED SELF

*"You are a sacred master divine being, and to
believe anything other than that is untrue. It is
not from an egotistical, self-centered, or conceited
way but the truth within your being with love.
The sacred self is the soul-centered self."*

—THEO

CAN YOU IMAGINE the possibility that happiness might be over-rated? Don't get us wrong, we love being happy as much as anybody, but maybe happiness is not the goal, maybe there is something that feels even better, that is a permanent state of being—a vibrational frequency of present moment awareness, fueled by gratitude—that becomes our new normal. A state that is not conditional on anything external happening to us, or for us, or if or when something happens, as is often the case when we experience temporary feelings of happiness.

And what if this state of being is who we really are, and that we are just now remembering, awakening, to our true nature—our sacred self?

This state of being, and our true nature is unconditional love, and that any beliefs we hold about ourselves that are not aligned with the vibration of unconditional love are simply not true. Together, we will begin now to discover how to change them—easily and permanently.

The state of being of unconditional love is not a feeling or an emotion. It is a way of being that brings great comfort, emotional mastery, peace, joy, abundance, clarity, spiritual connection, and yes, happiness. Happiness that is not conditional upon anything happening to make you feel that way. It's just the way you are.

So, what does this have to do with The Art of Relationship? Pretty much everything, as the relationship to yourself, the amount of love you have for yourself (making it possible to truly love others), coupled with the amount of love you allow yourself to receive, will determine the quality of all the relationships in your life. And you can't give or receive that which you don't already feel for yourself.

So, are you ready to embark on a journey of self-discovery, to know who you really are, to understand why you believe, think, and act the way you do, to change beliefs and patterns that no longer serve you, to establish and maintain healthy boundaries and to love yourself in a way that feels so good you may have a difficult time describing it?

To respond calmly to anything life throws at you, instead of reacting emotionally. To live in the present moment with no thoughts of regrets from the past or worries for the future.

A time of magic and miracles. Of the extraordinary becoming your new ordinary.

A time of creating soulfully connected relationships!

As THEO is an unlimited source of wisdom, the depth and breadth of THEO' teachings are limited only by our imagination, intellect, and curiosity, and by the quality of the questions we ask. Many who have had the opportunity to speak with THEO personally comment on how THEO seems to hold us in our highest light, as they see us only in our highest potential without any of the perceived limitations of situations and circumstances that might hold us back from living a life we love. As they have said to many "If you could see yourselves as we see you, there would be no discontent, only joy and love."

Imagine how wonderful your life—and your relationships—would be if you see and know yourself as THEO does!

MARCUS: Sheila, please share with us how THEO comes into your physical body. What does it feel like when they enter, and where do you go?

SHEILA: Well, I step aside. They have always come in the right side of my body, first taking over my neck, my head, my vocal cords, and then they take over the rest of my body. I have been doing this for so many years, so it is comfortable now for me to allow them to do that.

MARCUS: Are you ready to invite THEO in?

SHEILA: I am. It takes just a moment for me to move over and invite THEO in. So here we go. (Sheila closes her eyes and goes into trance. When she opens them about 10 seconds later, THEO begins to speak)

THEO: *"It is the beginning, is it not?"*

MARCUS: It is. Welcome, THEO.

THEO: *"We are appreciative of the opportunity to be of service unto you. You may ask."*

MARCUS: We are grateful to have you with us, THEO. Would you please introduce yourselves?

THEO: *"We are twelve archangelic beings collectively speaking by the name THEO, as the identification. We are here as mentors, teachers, and guides for a new time of consciousness for the human species, assisting this planet in the change to the 5th dimensionary energy, fully embracing the masters that you are."*

MARCUS: How is it that you speak through Sheila's physical body?

THEO: *"We have an agreement, and we align ourselves vibrationally with the frequency on the cellular level of this physical structure so that we may speak directly through her vocal cords to impart the knowledge for humanity."*

MARCUS: And why now?

THEO: *"Now is a time that has never before been on this planet, as we spoke of the 5th dimensionary energy fully in place on this planet now. It has taken a hundred years of adjustment to the planet and to the vibrations that align in the multidimensional field of which you, as the human beings, are aligning to that vibrational frequency as well. The 3rd dimension is your physical reality, the 4th is a spiritual awakening, and the 5th is the full realization of your divine mastery.*

MARCUS: What is your message for humanity right now regarding relationships?

THEO: *"It is all about love . . . Ask 'What would love do?' It is also the relationship to the self, first and foremost. You have heard these words before over time, but now is the time for that recognition, of Soul Integration, meaning, that there is a recognition of unconditional* *love of Self. And it is not a feeling. It is a state of being. It is that state of being of alignment, soul-centered, and expressing and responding to life from that state, not reacting to life from these fragmented aspects of the soul."*

MARCUS: What are the biggest mistakes you see us making in relationships?

THEO: *"There is a lack of communication, and there is a great fear of abandonment that drives one's interaction with another."*

MARCUS: A while ago, we asked you what aspect of your teachings you wanted us to focus on sharing with humanity, and you immediately said relationships. Why this topic?

THEO: *"Because that is what governs everything that you do. The relationship for the self first and how you believe in your self-worth drives what happens to you in life. So first, and most importantly, it is the relationship to the self, for that is reflective in everything, in all relationships—primary relationships, family relationships, work relationships, friendships. It is the beliefs about self that drive how one interacts with others."*

MARCUS: You have called this time that we are living in right now the 5th dimension. Can you explain?

THEO: *"It is a vibration. It is a frequency that permeates your atmosphere. There are 12 dimensions about the earth plane. And in the 5th dimension, the veils, let us say, between your multidimensionality are thinner. There is a recognition of all that you have been, all that you will be, and all that you are now that can be achieved in the inner process and an understanding of the self that is ever evolving. Now is the time of consciousness evolution that has not happened before on this planet."*

MARCUS: When you talk about the veils thinning between the dimensions, THEO, what does that mean?

THEO: *"That you have a familiarity with the concept of no time. You are attached to linear time because that is what dictates your daily activities and your day and night, and months—you have calendars* *for that and clocks for the time—but ultimately, that is just a way of navigating in life. But there is no time. All exists energetically in the now."*

MARCUS: **THEO, as twelve archangels never embodied, how is it that you are so wise in the realm of human relationships?**

THEO: *"We are good observers. We observe you interacting with each other, and understand this . . . we come from that solid state of love. That is what God is, you see. So, there is no judgment. We are aware that you choose incarnations for the gifts and the learnings therein, and the primary learning is emotions."*

MARCUS: **Who or what is our soul?**

THEO: *"It is the energy of that solid state of love."*

MARCUS: **And who or what is God?**

THEO: *"Unconditional love."*

MARCUS: **You talk about unconditional love being a state of being. Can you explain that, please?**

THEO: *"It is a state of being, not a feeling. It is how, when you are soul-centered, there is no reactivity, and it is only responding to outside situations, circumstances, and conditions, not reacting. Reacting comes from the emotional body and the fragmented aspects of the soul."*

MARCUS: **When you look at us, THEO, what do you see?**

THEO: *"If you could see yourselves as we see you, there would be no discontent, for we see you as the divine beings that you are."*

MARCUS: **How do you see our planet, THEO?**

THEO: *"We see it exquisitely. It has great beauty, and we see the beauty of the planet through your eyes."*

MARCUS: **Does our soul have an essence or an archetype? And when we reincarnate, do we have that same essence expressed in each lifetime?**

THEO: *"It is energy, you see. Everything is energy. You do have an expression of that energy, and some are artists and others are healers and others are leaders of spirit, others are political, if you would,* or warriors. There are different aspects in which an individual soul chooses incarnations that express those qualities of vibrations."

MARCUS: **So, we tend to show up with the same interests, the same skill sets, from lifetime to lifetime?**

THEO: "Yes. Or desires. That is why oftentimes there may be someone in a profession such as a medical profession, which is also an art, but then would desire to do music or writing to express in that way."

MARCUS: **How do you define love?**

THEO: "It is different for everybody, isn't it? Their own personal definition. That is why we encourage you to get into the solid state of unconditional love, and many know not what that means. There are different forms of love, are there not? There is a love of the material things. Some people love their automobile. Some people love each other. But that is only a projection of what they feel about themselves—expectations gone unmet to fulfill what one perceives is love is projected onto every relationship."

MARCUS: **And the most important love of all would be the love of self, wouldn't it?**

THEO: "Yes. For when one is soul-centered in that state of unconditional love, one can love another in that same essence."

MARCUS: **One of the definitions of self-love in Wikipedia is: "moral flaw, akin to vanity and selfishness, synonymous with amour propre, conceit, conceitedness, egotism, et al." It appears that many have adopted that definition.**

THEO: "That is because it has been misconstrued or judged by others. We are not speaking of narcissism, egocentric points of view, self-absorption, or conceit. All those things are personality disorders, aren't they? It is not the pure state of love of which we speak, and that love is compassion for every being."

MARCUS: **Why is it that so many people have such a difficult time loving themselves?**

THEO: "They have adopted beliefs about themselves that are simply untrue through situations, circumstances, conditions, and opinions of others. But understand this, if someone is judging you, they are seeing you through the lenses they see themselves, and they project that onto you."

MARCUS: **You have said before that we are an aspect of God/ Source. Please explain.**

THEO: "You are. Understand this, you are God incarnate. You are all that existing energy, the divine masters that you are expressing in a human condition—that solid state of love. What would love do? It is only through the human experience that one adopts a different opinion, you see, through the 3rd and 4th dimensional realities that there have been ways, and beliefs, that ones have adopted in the human experience that have been quite harsh and have nothing to do with love—but have to do only with survival."

MARCUS: **What do you mean when you ask "What would love do?"**

THEO: "Compassion. When you ask the self, 'What would love do?' it is a different perception that is achieved in any situation or circumstance. There is a different perception from reaction to responsiveness, a relinquishment of judgment of one another."

MARCUS: **We tend to have a difficult time owning that we are divine beings—that we are, in fact, an aspect of God.**

THEO: "It is because you have been taught not to think that because those who have taught you that wished to control you, to make you lesser than."

MARCUS: **I have heard you say many times that to not love our Self is arrogant. Please explain.**

THEO: "Because the gift of who you are incarnate is that essence of God, the brilliance of your magnificence, which you relinquish with those beliefs of not loving the self. So, you think you know better than God your intellect, your human expression? It does not."

MARCUS: **What is the path for us to love ourselves?**

THEO: "Through the soul integrative process. Acknowledge those little ones inside of you that influence the beliefs that you are not enough, you are not worthy. Communicate with them, the adult self. The *future self can even communicate with these little aspects that hold beliefs that limit you. Rewrite that script, and love and re-pattern the aspects of self that have held those limiting beliefs."*

This is the first reference THEO makes to Soul Integration, their multidimensional process for identifying the core circumstance, or event, that occurred (usually earlier in this lifetime or during a previous incarnation) during which an untrue and typically unloving or limiting belief about the self was created and adopted as truth going forward in our lives. This aspect of our Self/Soul (which THEO refers to as a fragment or an orphan) carries these untrue and unloving beliefs about ourselves throughout our lives and typically shows up as fear, resistance, emotional reactivity, lack of trust, poor relationships, limiting thinking, and an inability to take the necessary steps to manifest our dreams and desires. Understanding and implementing THEO's teachings on Soul Integration creates an awareness that any belief we hold about ourselves that is not unconditionally loving is simply not true. This is the first step toward becoming the vibrational state of being of unconditional love that THEO is exalting us to embrace now. Much more to come on this in the next chapter.

Maria, bless her brave soul, was understandably nervous about raising her hand to speak with THEO in front of a live audience. We applaud her courage for doing so, and for expressing her vulnerability and self-awareness, and for asking a question that we think each of us can relate to on some level. Maybe you will even see a little bit of yourself in Maria. One benefit of this process is how quickly the awareness of when and how the belief of unworthiness was created can lead to an immediate shift in our sense of well-being and confidence as you will see happen for Maria.

THEO LIVE WITH MARIA

MARIA: The main reason why I am up here is because I was afraid to come up. So, I knew that was a big reason to come, and so I am a little nervous. I am shaking. It is hard for me to hold it, and the reason is lack of self-worth. I feel that I am not worthy to be up here, but I really do want to be here.

THEO: "And you should be up here. And you are worthy of it. Close your eyes. It is not the adult self of you that feels unworthy. Who inside of you feels not worthy of being seen and heard? How old is she?"

MARIA: The five-year-old.

THEO: "Yes. You are aware of a circumstance, a situation, where she knew not to speak, to not be seen, to hide. It was safer there. Run down the hall. Slam the door. Hide behind it. The adult, you can call her out now and tell her it is safe. She does not have to be afraid anymore. You will take care of her. She does not have to take care of everything. It is not her job. You can do it together. She is not alone. Is she coming out? How does she feel?"

MARIA: She feels better.

THEO: "Continue the dialogue in letting her know that you are in charge. You will take care of her. You are the best parent for her. And you would like for her to come with you in the new life that is emerging for you both, now. Ask her if she wants to come."

MARIA: For some reason, I feel like I having trouble getting to her.

THEO: "It is about trust. She does not trust anybody. So, what you will be doing is building trust with her. Tell her it is all right. Let her know how good it is to be the woman you are now, how strong you are, and how she assisted you to be this person you are today, and you appreciate and love her . . . her strength. Her response?"

MARIA: We can do this.

THEO: "Is she ready?"

MARIA: Yes.

THEO: "Tell her you will not abandon her, and she does not have to *do things by herself anymore. You will take care of it. And she can always be heard by you and have a voice and speak her truth. She does not have to be afraid anymore. What is her response?"*

MARIA: She feels safe.

THEO: *"Ask her if it is all right if you come back now, to this moment, and come again and speak with her later. When you feel comfortable open your eyes. You made a connection, yes?"*

MARIA: Yes.

THEO: *"You are not shaking anymore, are you?"*

MARIA: No, I am not.

THEO: *"That is who shakes. That is who becomes afraid. Runs down the hall to hide in life. It is not the adult you, not the person that is the wise you. So, when you feel that, communicate with her. She is just reacting, and when you say to her, 'I am here. I will take care of it. We will do it together,' you will feel this calm you feel now, because she thinks she has to take care of everything. She can be the child, and you can take care of the adult things. You have many good skills, great skills, intuitive skills. This aspect of you assisted in developing these skills. That is what kept her safe. You can acknowledge her for that, and they will continue to grow. You don't have to be afraid anymore."*

MARIA SHARES HER EXPERIENCE

This was not just a conversation with THEO, it was the beginning of a spiritual healing and a shift into awakening. The 'knowing' I had deep within me, yet doubted for so long, had surfaced into my direct consciousness. All fear and uncertainty were transmuted. In that moment, I realized that everything I ever wanted, what is most important to me; happiness, love, family, and purpose is something I already have—right here, right now.

I discovered that it is the little one who carries the fear, worry and anger. I was given the most valuable tool to use when the little one feels reactive in a situation. It holds the key to my soul truth, happiness, and spiritual freedom.

Since my conversation with THEO, my life has changed drastically. I have developed a connec-tion with the little one inside and she has been guiding me through difficult times. She inspires me to keep going and to trust more and more each day. She is the reason why I am where I am, and I am grateful for that. It has been an empowering journey and it is unfolding perfectly. It is an experience I will never forget."

MARCUS: **Beliefs can also originate from experiences in previous incarnations, not just from this lifetime. It is multidimensional.**

THEO: *"It is multidimensional, and you are carrying forward from other times a desired outcome of learning and letting go of the old, to build on the new, to have the awareness of that divine essence."*

MARCUS: **What is the process of incarnating, and why do our souls choose to come into physical form?**

THEO: *"It is birth to birth, you see, and it is a soul's choice to do it. There are billions of choices that a soul can make. The Earth is only one. In your universe, there are billions of planets that you could choose that could sustain life, and we are only speaking of one universe. There are billions of universes as well. So, you limit your thinking to just this one place being all there is. So, a soul chooses the earthly plane for the learning of the emotions and the interactions with one another in the physical existence, and your earth suit, your physical body, in which you enter to navigate this earthy plane is a gift. It is miraculous actually."*

MARCUS: **Why do you see us having chosen this time in history to incarnate?**

THEO: *"It is that evolution of consciousness. One might call it a quantum leap, if you would, of awareness that allows for that now."*

MARCUS: What is our purpose for being here?

THEO: *"Being alive. That is very purposeful. You chose it—chosen to be all that you can be. What you are looking for is how to express the energy that you are with passion."*

MARCUS: How do we find that?

THEO: *"You know it. You go within. What are you attracted to? What are the ideas and imaginations you have of the expenditure of time? What would you do with your time? What would you love to do with those precious moments of life? That will indicate, that will direct you to expressing your passion."*

MARCUS: What would you say to those who do not feel inspired or do not feel tapped into what their passion is?

THEO: *"Dig a little deeper on the inner. What we mean by that is when you say you do not have it or you have gone numb to it, it is because these little aspects of self that hold the beliefs that you are not worthy and have adopted a belief that your passion—the thing you would love to do—is not possible because you have been told you are incapable of it, which is simply untrue."*

MARCUS: So, we judge ourselves based on others' opinions of us that are untrue. Are we also judging ourselves when we realize we are judging others?

THEO: *"When you have an opinion about someone, it is often a judgment, and that which you judge in another is a part of you as well. Everyone tries to avoid uncomfortable feelings and only accepts those that are more comfortable, but know they are all significant feelings. The experience of feelings is physical, visceral. You have a feeling, and it travels through your body in the nervous system and enters your brain. Your brain deciphers it and then decides how it is going to process and emote it—energy in motion. So, you confuse them as being the same because they are closely aligned, but emotions are not feelings. The feeling is a visceral experience in the nervous system that then gives information to your brain, and the brain is what emotes."*

MARCUS: And it is important that we own those feelings, to feel those feelings, to not resist them.

THEO: "Yes. Because if you are not expressing them, they become subverted in the physical body and can create imbalance—illness, disease—because it is held in the cellular structure of the body. So, to process them is what is important, and it does not need to be devastating. Know that if you acknowledge that they are there, you experience the experience and then it is released."

MARCUS: In talking about self-love, THEO, what do you see as the biggest mistake we make?

THEO: "By believing things that are untrue about yourself."

MARCUS: I think a lot of people perceive it as being too difficult, or impossible, to change our beliefs.

THEO: "You have given your power away to the opinions of others, and that has meant survival, for the greater fear in everyone is abandonment. And that is why you accept these beliefs as your own—because it allows you to survive in the environment that you are in, in that moment threatening you where the fear is so great. Do you understand?"

MARCUS: I do. When you look at human beings and how we interact with each other, how would you define a soulful connection?

THEO: "It is a vibrational frequency. It is a match. You are aligned with your vibrations and frequencies, and in that alignment, you have similar thoughts, similar beliefs, similar codes of conduct, you might say, personal code, core values."

You have probably heard it said many times that you cannot give what you do not have. There is a good reason why adults with small children must put the oxygen mask on themselves first, then the child second in the event of an emergency on an airplane. The same is true with love for it is difficult to genuinely love another if you do not first love yourself. What we enjoyed about the following conversation with THEO and Linda is how the love that Linda felt for her friends revealed a surprisingly deep love for herself—a recognition of being her own best friend—for had that not been the case, she would have been incapable of feeling such love with her friends.

THEO LIVE WITH LINDA

LINDA: So, I was curious about self-love and the difference between that and loving someone else. I was with my friends yesterday, and I had so much love. I was feeling like a dog wagging its tail, feeling mellow. But I was so happy to be with my buds, and it was just this huge love thing. I do not recall really feeling that with myself. I was curious that maybe in a deep state of meditation, there would be a different kind of love that maybe I have experienced before.

THEO: *"You are learning how to experience that on those levels of self and how you can know that is that you have felt it with your friends and your friends are but a reflection of you. And the love they have for you, you accept it. When you are with those who understand you and accept you for who you are, that reflects what you are doing on the inner. And that is why you felt joy because you felt loved and accepted. They know you very well and you know they know you very well, all of you, and they love you, and you them. That is what unconditional love is."*

LINDA: And that is like that endorphin rush when you are in love with a partner.

THEO: *"Yes. It brings out the best in you because that is who you truly are."*

LINDA: So, relationships are very serving in that way.

THEO: *"Yes."*

LINDA: It is hard to do that just for yourself if you are all alone.

THEO: *"Correct. You can be right that you are as bad as you think you are, yes?"*

LINDA: Right. So, coming together with another person, whether it is friendship, intimacy, or whatever, it makes that love express.

THEO: "Yes. It is better not to be neutral in that, yes?"

LINDA: No way!

THEO: "It is good to be human."

LINDA: Yes. Okay. Nice! Thank you, THEO.

LINDA SHARES HER EXPERIENCE

This experience with THEO reminded me that through the soul integration process, I have been able to develop an unconditionally loving relationship with myself.

THEO has shown me how to appreciate and acknowledge the person I am today, my gifts, talents, skills, strengths, and achievements small and great. This is my foundation, which is ever expanding.

I have learned the importance of cultivating myself on all levels. It is like tending a garden daily; caring for the physical, emotional, and spiritual aspects of my inner garden. Knowing what to water and fertilize, what needs to be weeded out—which plants need more tending, more attention. It is seeing the whole garden—my internal landscape—holistically.

My internal state is constantly growing, evolving, responding to all conditions. It is not about being 'perfect'. It is not about being perfectly grounded or centered all the time. It is loving the self during times of imbalance, loving the self enough to find balance again.

It is acknowledging and understanding inner confusion as it arises; the insecurities, doubts, fears, whatever shows up. Not judging one's faults or weaknesses. "I see you; I hear you, and there is love for you here." Always keeping the light in my heart temple burning bright, so when state of confusion arises, I have the tools to investigate the root cause, soothe and integrate.

It is really knowing and loving oneself; being real. All this allows room for growth. Growth can be messy, and it is a process; and I have learned to trust the process. In trusting and honoring myself, and my journey, the pressure to be 'perfect' is relieved. In a state of authenticity there is humility, empathy, and compassion for others and myself.

To unconditionally value all parts of myself, without judgment, blame or shame is me being my own best friend. The relationship I have with myself is most important. A relationship based on honesty, compassion, kindness, patience, love and respect, courage, perseverance, and taking responsibility. All this is what THEO's soul integration teachings have given me.

CHAPTER THREE

SOUL INTEGRATION— THE PATH TO LOVING YOURSELF

"Bringing together those fragmented aspects of the soul that hold unloving beliefs and releasing those beliefs in alignment with one's divine self. The soul-integrated self is aligned with the solid state of unconditional love."

—THEO

FROM WIKIPEDIA: Self-love, defined as "love of self" or "regard for one's own happiness or advantage",[1] has been conceptualized both as a basic human necessity[2][3] and as a moral flaw, akin to vanity and selfishness,[4] synonymous with amour propre, conceitedness, egotism, narcissism, et al.

Basic human necessity or moral flaw—Which version of self-love were you raised to believe? Many are raised to believe the latter—that it is conceited to "love yourself" and maybe you were even taught that you were born with something called original sin, an idea originated by St. Augustine (354–430), who wrote, "No one is free from sin, not even an infant whose span of earthly life is but a single day." How are you supposed to love yourself believing that you must have done something so wrong before you were even incarnated to be labeled a sinner for the rest of your life?

In the previous chapter, THEO introduced us to the concept of soul integration as the path to loving yourself. Simply put, this is a deep dive into discovering who you are, why you believe, think, and act the way you do, what core circumstances occurred whereby limiting beliefs about yourself were adopted, and how you can change those beliefs, thus changing the entire trajectory of your life. Limiting beliefs become empowered beliefs. Unloving beliefs become loving beliefs, and feelings of not being enough become feelings of confidence and courage. Your view of your world begins to change as the source of the beliefs fueling feelings of fear, resistance, and lack of trust are identified and re-patterned. You take the steps to pursue your dreams and begin to respond to life as an observer instead of reacting to life emotionally. Your relationships become more joyous and fulfilling. You become extremely comfortable in your own skin. Enhanced awareness, consciousness. It is that powerful.

Yet it is simple, too. Many say it reminds them of an inner child, or shadow, work of psychological models. And it is that. Many also say that it reminds them of soul retrieval work in the shamanic traditions. And it is that, too. The additional facet that makes this so transformative is that it is also a multidimensional process, incorporating memories and knowledge from previous incarnations that influence our emotional patternings in this lifetime. To tap into the knowledge contained in your full soul [some call it the akashic records], accessing ancient memories, and remembering more of who you are, for as THEO said in the last chapter, "The veils between the dimensions are now thinner than they have ever been in human history."

MARCUS: You have said that once we genuinely love ourselves, everything changes, and that soul integration is the path to creating this state of being. What is soul integration, and why is it so important?

THEO: "It is the process in which you can communicate with these little aspects of self that hold these limiting beliefs. For in those events, those moments where the belief is adopted or created, that part of self is frozen in that moment. So, the integrative process is that it thaws out the moment and allows that part of self to move forward into the present with you."

MARCUS: Does that freeze-framing stem from the essential need for survival?

THEO: "It does, yes. It is when the higher self steps in to take over when trauma is happening and responding to what is in that moment, you see.

MARCUS: How do you define the higher self?

THEO: "It is all that you are. It is the vibrational frequency of the entirety of your soul."

MARCUS: So, remembering the core circumstance from which an untrue belief about the self was created—and this could be in this lifetime or others—creates the awareness for where the belief began, and with that awareness, we are able to shift it, to move from a limiting to empowered belief about ourselves. Is that correct?

THEO: *"It is. It gives you information. It is revelatory. 'Ah, now I know where this began' and you, the adult self, can soothe and comfort and reframe, reparent that part of self that was frozen in that moment, giving love and support and security, and assurance that you will never abandon it."*

MARCUS: A lot of beliefs seem to be created primarily from our childhood years in this lifetime. I know there are other times in our life that this occurs as well, but these beliefs about ourselves often begin at an early age, don't they?

THEO: *"Yes, even in utero at times. So, it is to understand that because the body is small, even as a fetus, does not mean that the soul is."*

MARCUS: Speak more to that, please.

THEO: *"So there is a tendency to think that an infant or a toddler or a young child, because their body is young and the body is smaller, that their soul is young also and lacks understanding. Know that the soul is so much larger than you can imagine."*

MARCUS: A lot of people, when they hear about your soul integration process, say it sounds like the inner child work of psychological models, as well as the soul retrieval work of shamanic traditions. But it is more than that, isn't it?

THEO: *"It is. It addresses your multidimensionality, whereas the inner child work addresses only the present incarnation."*

MARCUS: Please expand.

THEO: *"You are a multidimensional soul. You are the total of all your experiences in the human experience, you see, and more. So, the soul chooses an incarnation to achieve a particular learning and that desire for learning comes from other experiences that it has had while previously embodied. So, it chooses an incarnation in which to express that. It is similar in energetics so that one can move and up-level, if you would, to experience that education."*

MARCUS: What is the significance of understanding previous incarnations? A lot of us were raised with religious beliefs that did not even allow for the possibility of past lives. So, is there a shift in that belief that is required to embrace this process?

THEO: "Yes, but anywhere in the Bible, you can find facts to support your beliefs, for Jesus spoke of this, and other master teachers have as well from other religious events or celebrations."

MARCUS: Jesus taught reincarnation?

THEO: "Yes, but others would differ that he did not. So, it is always an argument in belief, isn't it?"

MARCUS: It is. So, speaking of the beliefs that we adopt from previous incarnations, what if we can only access the feelings? If we have a feeling of an experience as opposed to a specific memory, is that enough to create the awareness needed to be able to shift that belief?

THEO: "Yes, it is. Trust your knowing. Your intuitive knowing is very strong, and you all have evidence about that as truth, for you have evidence in life where you have trusted it, and whatever you have been given has been proven correct. You have been affirmed and confirmed in it. So, you do have some evidence of this to build on, do you not?"

MARCUS: We do, but we seem to be tough on ourselves and are challenged to believe that we can shift these beliefs of not feeling loveable enough. Why is that?

THEO: "It is an experiential process. It is not an intellectual process."

MARCUS: So, what is the source of low self-esteem?

THEO: "It is a belief of not being good enough—not pretty enough, not handsome enough, not smart enough, whatever it is that others have visited upon you and you accepted as truth. It is always coming outside of you, which then on the inner levels, you allow to diminish you."

MARCUS: And it leads to repeating self-sabotaging behaviors.

THEO: "Until you don't. Until you realize that that is just a pattern to prove that belief correct. When you have an understanding of where the core issue began, that revelation that we spoke about, that is where you begin shifting that pattern, rewriting the script, loving that part of self forward into the now."

MARCUS: So, what we are really talking about here is awareness. That just having that awareness of the memory, or the feeling, allows us to respond differently without having to repeat the same behavior?

THEO: "It is awareness, and then, it is a process of love, isn't it?"

MARCUS: Speak more to that.

THEO: "Loving the self. Loving that part of self, letting it know it will always have a voice with you. You will not abandon it. Encouraging it to come with you into the new life that you are creating now, out of the moment in time where they were frozen in that experience."

MARCUS: Once we have an awareness of this, how do we then transform that belief into a more empowering belief about ourselves?

THEO: "By speaking the truth of it. It is a reframing of the event, reprogramming, if you would. Events will not change. That is history. Whatever has happened to you in life that has created a belief of your unworthiness, whatever it was, harsh or not, whatever has happened will not change. Your perception of it can change. Your perception of it can change in an instant when you realize the gifts and the blessings in each experience that the soul has given you and moving forward into the now."

MARCUS: Is there anything you can add as it relates to making these beliefs a permanent part of us moving forward?

THEO: "You do by living them and having the awareness each time there is a reactivity from this aspect of self. All it is asking is to be heard, to be seen, to be loved. So, if you are reactive and they are the reactor, then acknowledge them, letting them know that they will not be abandoned, they are safe, and you will take care of them."

MARCUS: Please speak about beliefs that are created from an abusive childhood in this lifetime. A child that did not grow up feeling loved.

THEO: *"So there are patterns that show up in life where one attracts another out of that woundedness. Then there is a repetition of that lack of love with individuals that are like them, that have no ability or awareness of how to love. It is magnetic in that way."*

"Like attracts like" and "Birds of a feather flock together" are just two of the common ways to describe THEO's statement that ". . . it is magnetic in that way." We are energy beings, each with our own unique vibrational frequency, that attract those of a similar vibration. As we change our beliefs and thoughts, we change our vibration and attract to ourselves those who also think and believe as we do. The Law of Attraction, as THEO says, is always working perfectly, and this is one example of how it works.

Judy's story and her experience with THEO inspired us greatly. Her story is an amazing example of how transformation can occur by asking highly calibrated questions and making the decision to not allow her conditions and circumstances, or her upbringing, determine the quality of her life going forward. You will also see how magnetic attraction works in manifesting similar relationships over and over until we make the decision to change.

One of the most poignant moments in Judy's experience is when she recognizes that the younger fragmented aspects of herself/soul—created out of the need for survival—in fact, contributed significantly to her surviving in life and becoming the strong woman she is today. Having gratitude for this recognition is one of the keys to the integration. You may also notice that soul integration is a process where deeply held beliefs and building trust can take some time. However, when the awareness occurs, it will be with you your entire life, allowing you to permanently shift from being reactive to being responsive to life circumstances.

THEO LIVE WITH JUDY

JUDY: I am interested in knowing the steps to love myself. I see that is the way to have a better life, a life fulfilled, when you talk about my best life, and like that man said, "Why waste time not living my best life anymore?"

THEO: "Good."

JUDY: I need help figuring out how to do that.

THEO: *"In just asking the question, it has already begun, and you felt the fear, and you stepped into anyway."*

JUDY: Yes, thanks to Maria. She really inspired me to just go ahead and come up here.

THEO: *"Good. We do not bite. We do work on your energy, however, so you may feel the vibrations going through your body. Do not be afraid of them. We are just opening you up. Close your eyes. It is not the adult you that is afraid, and you know that to be true. Who is it?"*

JUDY: It just feels endless. I don't know. It is probably a lot of parts of me. I just don't know. My mom was starving when she was pregnant with me. I know that.

THEO: *"Breathe."*

JUDY: I know that when I was five, I was sent away, and I know that I have abandonment issues. I know that. I cried and quit eating until they sent me back to my mom, but it was a hard life. I had teenage parents. I guess my soul picked them as my parents in this lifetime to go through all of this. But I am tired of it now. I just want to be balanced.

THEO: *"So, let's talk to this little girl. We are going to your future self now because you are immersed, the adult you, is immersed emotionally right now with this little one. Breathe. We, and your future self, are talking to the five-year-old now. Ask her what she needs from you, for you are the best parent for her. You can give her everything that she needs. Let her know that she is loved, and you won't abandon her."*

JUDY: I know that, but there are trust issues.

THEO: "Of course, she does not trust. What if she is sent away again? That is her greatest fear. Tell her that you will take care of her. She does not have to be afraid. The adult, that is you, has the strength to care for her. Let her know how strong you are because of her. You survived incapable parents. You are here."

JUDY: Wow! That is amazing she has survived, and with giving strength for my adult self. That is beautiful.

THEO: "Yes. Tell her how much you love her for that strength."

JUDY: Wow.

THEO: "And you will take care of her. She can trust you to do that, and she will always have a voice with you. Breathe. How does she feel?"

JUDY: I am trying to talk to her now, so I am now focusing on talking to her.

THEO: "Speak to her out loud."

JUDY: Okay.

THEO: "What would you say to her?"

JUDY: Don't be afraid. I will take care of you. I am strong enough to take care of you, and I will not leave you. I am here for you, and I will always be here for you. You will not be alone. I am here with you. I will not leave you alone.

THEO: "What is her response?"

JUDY: That feels good to know.

THEO: "You can see her and feel her, can't you? So, envision the house where you were raised. Where your mother left. Where you went back to. There is a front porch, and you are standing with her on the walkway in front of this house and behind you stretches a path to the new life where you come together and share life together now. That you are the best parent for her, and you will take care of her. Ask her if she wants to go with you down that path."

JUDY: She wants to know if it is okay to leave her mom.

THEO: "Of course, it is. That is what is going to happen next, and she will be just fine. She does not have to take care of the mother anymore.

You will take care of this little girl. She is your little girl. So, the mother is there on the porch, and you can say goodbye to her. That part is finished. It is complete. And you and she can turn around and face the direction of the new path, the new life, that is emerging for you both. Ask her if she wants to go."

JUDY: I am having a problem. I am getting a headache, and it feels a little traumatizing.

THEO: *"Breathe."*

JUDY: Okay. It is funny. It is like a reverse abandonment because my mom was always sad that she did not have her mom present, and so I guess this aspect of me feels guilty to leave her.

THEO: *"She is just fine."*

JUDY: Okay.

THEO: *"To be in integrity with your little one on the inside, you care for her now."*

JUDY: Okay.

THEO: *"It is not your job to be the mother for your mother. That is an inside-out process, which you are discovering. And, in truth, you are not leaving your mother behind, are you?"*

JUDY: No.

THEO: *"There is still that love, but what you are doing is taking this child with you, out of those moments of despair, into the new life of love and connectivity."*

JUDY: My little self is afraid of change, and that is why, in my lifetime, I have been stuck in relationships that are not good. I am having a hard time with my mom dying, with the divorce, because of the drastic changes. And I have a hard time adjusting, and so, that is part of the fear of any change of leaving my mom or changing anything in my life. But I want to do it anyways. I just need help with that fear.

THEO: *"That is what we are doing. So, it is not the adult you that is afraid of it. It is this little girl. So comfort her. What does she need from you to feel comfortable in making that change?"*

JUDY: Protection.

THEO: "You can give her that. You will take care of her. She is not alone. She has you, and you are not going to leave her."

JUDY: Right. Okay.

THEO: "How do you feel?"

JUDY: Better because she is protected.

THEO: "And you know better than anybody how to protect her."

JUDY: I am learning.

THEO: "Yes."

JUDY: The other thing is learning boundaries. That is part of the protection.

THEO: "She has been running the show. She has been running your life. The adult has not, so now the adult is in charge. So, let her know you love her and will not abandon her, and you will take care of all the adult things, and she can be the child. You are redefining your roles."

JUDY: Okay.

THEO: "How do you feel?""

JUDY: It feels really good.

THEO: "Good. There is relief, yes? Now you have made that connection, and when she reacts, you can talk to her again and just reassure her that she is loved and safe."

JUDY: You know that is new, a new learning.

THEO: "Of course, it is. That is why you are going to repeat it every day. In the night when you awaken and there are just these thoughts, give her a hug and tell her that it is okay. She can sleep, and she does not have to be afraid. And you will find you rest easier. It is a process that you have begun. And it is so, and it is done. Ask her if you can leave her now for this moment, to come again to speak with her in not too long of a time in this day. Ask her if it is all right if you come back here now."

JUDY: Yes.

THEO: "And when you are ready you can open your eyes and be back in this room."

JUDY: But I want to take her to that new direction that you talked about.

THEO: "Good. So, in a few moments, you can take her by the hand. Ask her how she wants to go to your new home."

JUDY: She wants to skip.

THEO: "Good. So, you can skip, yes? Excellent. Now you know . . . you are going to skip home. It is a good thing. So it is. So, you can take her with you to your seat. Tell her that you will be skipping and do it . . . skip down the hall. Nobody cares. Is it all right with her if you come back to this room for the moment? She can come with you."

JUDY: Yes.

THEO: "Good."

JUDY: I feel so much better now.

THEO: "Of course, you do. It has only just begun. You have the tools now. You know what to do, and you can do it. So it is."

JUDY SHARES HER EXPERIENCE

I was born and raised on Kodiak Island, Alaska, until I was twelve, and I had teenage parents. I am a female Native Alaskan from the Sugpiaq and Aleut tribes. My early childhood beliefs were shaped by the patriarchal, Christian, and white dominant society at the time, in the mid-1950s. So, it's no wonder I struggled all my life with self-esteem issues of feeling unworthy and undeserving. We were poverty stricken and discriminated against. Sadly, I suffered sexual abuse from male relatives and drunken strangers my mom took in who traveled to town by bush plane from the villages—to help with food and survival.

My first marriage ended in divorce after seven-and-a half years and left me struggling financially with joint custody of three little kids. I then entered an abusive relationship for 13 years until a therapist finally helped me to get out of it. And then I chose a homeless alcoholic hippie for my next boyfriend.

When my mom passed in 1995 at the age of 56 from cancer, my youngest child soon turned 18 and moved out. I suddenly found myself alone in the house for the first time. I broke up with the hippie boyfriend and quickly married a PTSD Vietnam veteran in 1996.

I became ill for three years and went to various doctors seeking a diagnosis and cure. That led me down a path of exploring energy healing. At first, I was just trying to heal my body, and after that was accomplished, I started learning how to heal my soul of childhood scars and wounds. And that has been a long but satisfying journey.

In October of 2019, I flew to Phoenix to attend the Art of Relationship weekend retreat with THEO. On Friday, the first night of the retreat, I was excited and nervous. When I witnessed other people brave enough to go up in front of the audience, I decided that I had to raise my hand before the weekend was over.

I was the last person picked on Saturday to talk to THEO. I cried through most of it, but the experience of interacting live with THEO was unforgettable and transformative! THEO actually walked up to me while my eyes were closed and helped me work through my emotional despair. For me, the audience disappeared, and I was just tuned in to THEO and what they were saying to me. They guided me through a soul integration experience of bringing home my five-year-old self to the present time and to my life now. What I found most interesting during that experience was the fact that I didn't want to "abandon" my mom because she had abandoned me at that age by sending me to a white family somewhere on an airplane to be adopted out, where I cried and quit eating, and so they sent me back to my mom. THEO reassured me that my mom was fine and had moved on.

Afterwards many folks in the audience approached me

and thanked me, because my interaction with THEO helped them with their own issues. After that experience with THEO, it feels to me like the world looks different! So many people said I looked different afterwards, and I still FEEL different! It's a miracle! It's indescribable. I feel so much more peace, love, and joy inside. I just do. Like NEVER in my life! I felt like I was floating long after I got back home! Ever since my experience with THEO, I feel complete. I mean I feel more whole within myself. I no longer feel the need to go out and seek something to fill me up. I feel content being here alone with myself. Just this incredible feeling of serenity. My gratitude is so deep for being able to have this life-changing experience with THEO, and to everyone involved that made it happen.

MARCUS: As we adopt these principles, what does our life begin to feel and look like? How does it affect our relationships?

THEO: *"So there is a process where the old relationships drop away and new ones are formed out of the new way of being and the new patterning that is the love within. For you learn how to love the self enough that you hold your boundaries, and soon, you do not attract one that is wounded, for you are no longer wounded in yourself."*

MARCUS: It is the new paradigm, isn't it?

THEO: *"It is."*

MARCUS: What more can you tell us about the new paradigm in relationships?

THEO: *"The new paradigm of relationship, the new patterning of relationship, is preferential, not needy. In the past, you needed each other to survive. The woundedness in one would attract the woundedness in another with the belief that if you took care of them, they would take care of you, which is impossible because it is from the inside that the healing occurs. It is something you give yourself, and* then, it is exhibited out into the world. And so, the old paradigm has been out of need, needing from the outside to be filled up, for expectations to be met, which is a vicious cycle, isn't it? For then, it creates a pattern of a belief, even deepening that belief that you are not worthy of unconditional love."

MARCUS: **How does this lead us to discovering and living our passion?**

THEO: "You are empowered by that recognition of your self-worth, and in that knowing, you can accomplish what you love and what you desire for the outcomes of life, no longer aligning to the limiting beliefs that if you are shining your divine light, it diminishes someone else, and it does not."

MARCUS: **We tend to not want to outshine others for acceptance's sake, don't we?**

THEO: "Yes, for acceptance's sake and love, and to not be abandoned because human beings, the human species, are herd animals. You want to belong to the herd, the tribe, the community, the family, whatever it is. To belong is safe; it means safety that you can survive. That is human nature. It is animal nature. Yes?"

MARCUS: **Yes, as you said, we are all herd animals.**

THEO: "Yes."

MARCUS: **With this awareness, we can then begin to develop a sense of self, a sense of our authentic self. And what does that mean— to be our authentic self?**

THEO: "Allowing all that you are to come forth. Being in your truth. The truth of who you are is the gift you give the world."

MARCUS: **Speak more to that.**

THEO: "Not giving your power away for acceptance's sake."

MARCUS: **And that is common, isn't it?**

THEO: "It is, yes, because you desire love. You desire to belong. And for many, you give your power away when you do not tell the truth. What we mean by telling the truth is, even in the small things, such as when a friend, someone you care about, asks you if you would like to have a meal and they suggest a certain type of food, let us say Italian, and that is not what you are interested in at the moment. You say, "Yes that would be perfect," which is not true because it is not what you want. Wouldn't it be better if you said to that friend or loved one, "That would not be my first preference of food. Could we decide on something we both would enjoy? I would love to have a meal with you." That is the truth. And said kindly, yes?"

MARCUS: Yes. I know that is a simple example, but it does reflect how we give our power away within relationships.

THEO: "That is just a simple example, but you say yes when you mean no."

MARCUS: I have heard you say that no is a sentence.

THEO: "So is yes."

MARCUS: No explanation needed?

THEO: "Correct because you are each divine master beings, and if you say no, you don't have to explain or have an excuse why that it is. Or even when you say yes, you are making a statement out of your own divine essence, which is your truth."

MARCUS: Tell us the difference between judgment and observation.

THEO: "Judgment always has an emotional connectivity. If you are judging someone, you have an emotional charge. There is something that is happening that you are reactive to. If you are observing a situation, it is neutral. Isn't that interesting?"

MARCUS: It is. Is emotional neutrality even possible?

THEO: "Neutrality is possible. For an example, if you are looking at a flower and notice it has pretty colors and it is something you like, you feel not emotional about it. Or you could if you like that particular flower a great deal, but most often it is a neutral noticing, isn't it? But if you look at it and have a reaction to it—that is an ugly color, I do not like that flower, whatever it is—there is an emotionality to that. So, you look for where the emotion is coming from, where the reactivity is coming from. Something inside of you is triggered with judgment."

MARCUS: You talk a lot about the adult self and the future self, and the fragmented aspects of self from which the beliefs originated. Talk to us about the adult self in the process that you are describing.

THEO: "The adult self is the noticer, the responder, who is non-emotional, while the fragmented soul aspect is the reactor, which is from the emotional body. It can be different ages in which a belief about the self was adopted and created, and it is being triggered by the energy of the person or circumstance in the present. So, there may be ages where that belief is becoming reaffirmed and confirmed of being right. So, when you are integrating you may find, as we call, the string of pearls—different ages that hold the same belief and reactivity. It begins at a core circumstance, and then, it is reaffirmed, for you attract on a vibrational level similar situations and circumstances to reaffirm those beliefs. That is what can be changed. The future self is that part of self that is in your dimensional expression, your multidimensional being, that has moved through a moment in time, your linear time, and has the wisdom of that moment to call upon.

MARCUS: So, the desired outcome is to be responsive to life's circumstances with compassion and non-judgment, as opposed to being reactive, because in that reactivity typically is a judgment of others and of ourselves, correct?

THEO: "Correct."

MARCUS: Speak more to that, please.

THEO: "So in the process of integration, as you are loving the self forward into the now, you will begin to notice the things that triggered you, off-put you, become less and less, and you begin to notice that you are not reacting as you did in the past to the same stimulus . . . that you are responding differently to life."

MARCUS: How do you define the ego? And what is the ego's role regarding what we are talking about?

THEO: "It is very necessary as part of the human experience, isn't it? The ego is a protector. It is a façade that one wears as a safety in the *world in its interactive process. So, it is not that you want to kill it. Many speak of getting rid of the ego. Why would you do that? It is a part of your human experience. Love it. It, too, changes as you change."*

MARCUS: **Is the ego driven by the fragmented aspects of the soul that you are talking about?**

THEO: *"Yes."*

MARCUS: **Always?**

THEO: *"Always."*

MARCUS: **Speak more to that.**

THEO: *"It is the sergeant of arms, you might say, the protector. So, you see at times when beings are showing or acting superior to others, it is only to cover over their inferior feelings of self. That is the ego."*

MARCUS: **THEO, when you talk about noticing what we are noticing, being the observer of our own thoughts, what does that mean, and how can we master that?**

THEO: *"Paying attention. It is in that noticing what you are noticing. It is not only about your thoughts. It is about your actions about what is occurring around you. It is with intention you live life and then pay attention. Pay attention to all the things that are occurring."*

MARCUS: **What aspect of our self is doing the observing, thinking the thought that I am now observing?**

THEO: *"The observer in you."*

MARCUS: **Who is that?**

THEO: *"It is part of the self, isn't it?"*

MARCUS: **Is it the more awakened or more aware part of ourselves, our higher self, that is interacting with our human self?**

THEO: *"It is all spiritual. You do not hang your soul in the closet or on the doorknob when you leave your home or go to work or anything that you are doing. It is all part of life, whatever you are doing, and it is all part of your spiritual path."*

MARCUS: **It sounds like the better we become at observing, the happier we are going to be in our lives.**

THEO: "It is how you observe. It is how you observe life. If you are observing from a judgmental point of view, that is not necessarily true. If you can be neutral in your observation, you can recognize that it is an opportunity for growth and what can be gained from any situation, circumstance. And what we mean by that is, what is the gift? What is the blessing to be given there in that experience? Whatever it is."

MARCUS: We have the tendency sometimes of thinking that life is happening to us, but the reality is that it is really happening for us, isn't it?

THEO: "Yes, and through you, not to you. You are the creator of life. It is happening for your behalf. You have chosen it, you see."

MARCUS: And there are some great learning experiences that we might not have consciously signed up for if we knew how difficult they were going to be.

THEO: "That is a perception as well, isn't it? How difficult it was going to be. It is all perception. Suffering is optional."

MARCUS: Let's talk about change. Why is it so difficult for most people?

THEO: "That is the only thing that you can know is a constant. If you are breathing, there is change. And so, when one resists change, what are you afraid of? It is a fearful reaction to the possibility of change. Faith and fear ask the same of you—to believe in something unseen. So why not have faith? For oftentimes, when you are fearful of something it is unrealized. It is just the what-if this or that, or it could be the expectation of what-if in an enthusiastic way of greeting life, of trusting and being in love with life."

MARCUS: How does the Soul Integration process create a greater chance of manifesting our dreams?

THEO: "It is by releasing beliefs that you do not deserve what your dreams are. To achieve them, you must love them and love the self and know that you are worthy of that accomplishment."

MARCUS: So, the Soul Integration process then creates less resistance and more trust.

THEO: "Yes, and there is an acceptance. 'I am the person who deserves to have my dreams and desires met. I am a divine master being that is creating a life well-lived.'"

MARCUS: THEO, what have I not asked about Soul Integration that you would like to share?

THEO: "It is a process and to not be afraid of it. For most beings think that if they unlock that box, they will discover that they are as bad as they think they are, and it is the opposite . . . You find your divine essence there."

CHAPTER FOUR

LOVING YOURSELF CHANGES EVERYTHING

"The love of Self is the greatest change that can occur for all the energy aligns on your behalf."

—THEO

IMAGINE BELIEVING, knowing without doubt, that any thought that was not unconditionally loving about yourself was simply not true. That any limiting, self-defeating notion of who you are originated from events, circumstances, or the projections of others that occurred earlier in this lifetime or another. What changes would you make? Is it possible you might take better care of yourself physically, eat better, meditate regularly, or get better sleep? Maybe quit thinking and speaking negative thoughts about yourself? By engaging with THEO's soul integration process, you may even feel more comfortable and pain-free in your physical body due to the enhanced awareness of how emotions manifest as pain and inflammation when not acknowledged or left unexpressed. Setting and maintaining healthy boundaries becomes much more comfortable, as you will no longer be making decisions based on the good opinions or approval of others. You are now speaking your truth, being authentic. Timeframes seem to collapse in the manifestation of your dreams and desires due to you believing that you are truly deserving of what you want; you are receptive and are no longer fearful to act when the opportunities show up. And for many, one of the most rewarding outcomes is the connection made with your angels, your higher self, your Source, because of you knowing that this connection is your natural birthright, not just for others with more psychic abilities, but for you.

You will also attract relationships that feel more joyous and fulfilling! Knowing who you are, having awareness, an understanding of the core circumstance from which a belief was created, to know why you believe, think, and act the way you do is incredibly empowering. You no longer must react emotionally to situations and circumstances that trigger you within relationships. You can now respond as an observer instead of reacting out of an old pattern that no longer serves you.

The following story from our good friend Christine, from Melbourne, Australia, perfectly Illustrates this last point. She began embracing THEO's Soul Integration teachings several years ago and shares an experience with her husband that illustrates how a single moment of awareness can change your behaviors forever, which also speaks to how accessing a memory from a previous lifetime can shift the dynamics significantly in your current one.

"I had been, for the last few months, integrating a fragmented part of myself, from a past life shared with my husband. That past life was traumatic for the both of us. In this current incarnation, we are not playing out the same roles, but there was a heavy emotional carryover, and I felt our marriage was very average and our communication basic. I also often thought I would be better off divorced than living with him.

"One morning during school holidays at the beach, our teenage children had already headed off with their friends, and my husband and I were preparing to meet up with them. My husband noticed the mess our kids had left behind, and he started to complain about it emphatically. Instantly, I felt my body go to my familiar, typical, visceral reaction of anger as I started to hold my breath. Simultaneously my mind took off. 'Oh great! There he goes again. What the **bleep** does HE WANT NOW? WHO THE **BLEEP** CARES?'

"I noticed both, **the anger** and **my words, matching that anger**. I caught them in action! As soon as those thoughts were thought I took a deep breath and lovingly told my fragmented part who uttered those words, 'No, we are not doing that anymore!' The following question surfaced: 'If I'm not doing that, then how do I respond?' The Soul answer that came forth was that there was no need to say anything to him directly. Instead, I got the vision to 'wrap him up in amethyst.' For my logical brain, this was an illogical response, but I did it anyway; I imagined him encased in beautiful amethyst. Later, I looked up the benefits of amethyst to discover it is a natural tranquilizer; it relieves stress and strain and soothes irritability. That was the best way to respond to him in **that** moment. It was also an act of assistance for him rather than my typical knee-jerk reaction of anger and criticism.

"A few years have passed now, since the miraculous moment, where I actively exercised choice. Looking back now, little did I know then that my 'No' would completely change the trajectory of my relationship with myself and my husband. Now, I am more peaceful and more centered, and my relationship with him has flourished greatly. A strong bond of trust and safety has developed between us where I express myself more freely and calmly, and the best thing is, there is way more fun and laughter too. Words cannot express how blessed I feel to have decided to take Theo's Soul Integration teachings and implement them into my day-to-day interactions."

MARCUS: I have heard you say many times that loving our Self changes everything. Please explain.

THEO: *"It changes perceptually. It changes how you view life and others. When you love yourself enough, you can manifest all dreams and desires, for there is no blockage or resistance for its acceptance."*

MARCUS: THEO, tell us about how loving ourselves affects all the relationships in our lives?

THEO: *"You are not reactive. It affects everything that you do because you are responsive to life, not reacting to it. Reaction is an automatic response to emotional triggers. So, when you have an integrated beingness, then you respond not out of fear or all the limiting thoughts but out of responsiveness to events and situations and circumstances from a calm, solid state of unconditional love."*

MARCUS: How do your Soul Integration principles affect our ability to manifest money?

THEO: *"It is all about beliefs. What do you believe about money? Money has no energy in and of itself. It is what your beliefs give it, and so, the integrative process allows you to recognize your self-worth surrounding money. And what that means is—what are the beliefs, what is the language, what have you incorrectly assumed about yourself and money that creates a resistance for receiving it?"*

MARCUS: **I have heard you say that money only goes where it is loved.**

THEO: *"Yes, everything goes where it is loved. The only time it does not arrive is when there is some inner resistance that pushes it away."*

MARCUS: **How can we know when there is resistance that pushes it away?**

THEO: *"How it feels. Are you triggered? If you are asking the question 'Why don't I have enough? Why don't I have the things that I want? I want more pay for my work'—whatever it is—the feeling of not enough is giving you feedback, universal energy-wise, that there is resistance there."*

MARCUS: **So, it invites us to look at whatever beliefs we have adopted about that.**

THEO: *"Yes. How do you speak about it? What is your self-speak about that and many other things? Pay attention to the words. Words are things, and they manifest. They have a powerful vibration."*

MARCUS: **Talk to us about the power of the "I am."**

THEO: *"The 'I am' is the God that you are. I am a divine master being. I am Marcus. When you say, 'I am' and give your name, it is the God of you that you are introducing. The 'I am' is the power of creation, so use it judiciously. Don't empower things that you don't want by saying the 'I am.'"*

MARCUS: **Talk about Soul Integration as it relates to our physical health. How can we work with these principles to optimize our health?**

THEO: *"So in your body, where is there is pain or imbalance, there is an emotional component—the spiritual and emotional component. Body-mind-spirit, that is what has been talked about for years and years, but the only thing that was paid attention to was the body. And it was only paid attention to when it was uncomfortable, giving you a message that there was something out of balance. But under-stand this, it all works together. So, the emotional components will pool energetically in the areas that are the weakest for the physical body, so then there is discomfort. Anytime you are uncomfortable— whether it is emotionally or physically—you can identify that it is part of the fragmentation of the soul speaking to you, that it wants to be heard."*

The following session with Anne illustrates how our self-love can be shaped for our entire lives when we grow up feeling unloved by a parent, in this case, her father. Patternings of not feeling enough guide our decision-making, even to the point of choosing partners with similar characteristics as our parents until we have an awareness that it no longer must be that way. Part of what inspires this awareness is when Anne realizes that her father did the best he could with his limited level of awareness while feeling a lack of love for himself. How could he show her love when he did not even know how to love himself? When this recognition occurs, there is often an "Aha" moment when we begin to feel compassion instead of anger or resentment, and the healing and forgiveness process begins.

THEO also reminds Anne that the reason she remains in a marriage that she wishes to leave is that she does not have a plan (yet), a vision of how the next chapter of her life is going to be. The more she continues to know herself as the divine, loveable woman that she is, the easier it is for that plan to materialize.

THEO LIVE WITH ANNE

ANNE: I really need some help with resistance and self-love. I want to open my heart, but it feels like a big boulder. And I guess I am stopping it because I am scared.

THEO: "It is protective. That is true."

ANNE: Okay. Do you see a health challenge with this?

THEO: *"With your closed heart?"*

ANNE: Yes. It is just like a big wall.

THEO: *"The challenge will be as it opens you may think it is a problem, but it is not. Your heart is all right. You may have a bit of uncomfortability as it opens, but it is not a heart issue. It is just your heart opening, and occasionally you will have a pain there. That is why you are asking us."*

ANNE: Yes.

THEO: *"But it is just part of that cracking open, if you would."*

ANNE: Will I turn around energetically? I feel like it has been a game I have been playing with myself for a few years now.

THEO: *"When you open, you will be completely open. And your heart will be filled, and there will be joy. A part of that fear is 'What if this happens and I'm still the same, that nothing changes?' You will change. It is changing as we speak."*

ANNE: Okay. I guess that was my concern. With the relationship I had with my dad, I just feel like I do not know how to forgive sometimes.

THEO: *"That is all right. It will come. There are some similarities between your husband and your father, and the immense anger that you have been able to exhibit to your husband is the anger that you felt at your father. But that is a realization. It is part of the heart opening that is happening, that clarity. What we are going to say about your father is that he was very wounded, and he did not know how to be any other way. He created a rigidity in him that he passed along to everybody around him, with expectations that were impossible to meet. You could never do anything right, could you?"*

ANNE: No.

THEO: *"Because he couldn't see himself in that light. So, if he couldn't, how could anybody else."*

ANNE: That is true. Okay, that makes sense. It is like my husband, too. I always feel like I am damned if I do and damned if I don't.

THEO: *"Yes. Because what is expected by them is something that they must do on the inside. Nobody can do anything for them."*

ANNE: I guess I am always trying to do it for them.

THEO: *"Yes. 'If I could love you enough, you could love me.' That is a subconscious expectation that kept being unmet. It is because it is impossible for them. They cannot meet it in themselves. They have no idea what that means. Do they want that kind of love for self? Everybody does but do not know how. It is like asking an apple tree to give you an orange. Do you see?"*

ANNE: Yes, it is impossible.

THEO: *"Yes."*

ANNE: Will my self love and judgment get better?

THEO: *"It has gotten better. Look how far you have come. Will it get bet-ter still? Of course, because you know more, and you will look in the mirror and see the change in you, the beauty that is emerging, the energy, the light, that is coming forth now. It will come whether you leave the marriage or not. You have put your foot upon that path; there is no going back. You have already known that to be true. You cannot go back to the old you. There is an ever-emergence of your true self that is coming forth, unencumbered from the past."*

ANNE: (Heavy exhale)

THEO: *" Good, you felt that."*

ANNE: Yes.

THEO: *"And that is the truth."*

ANNE: Thank you.

THEO: *"There is an asking?"*

ANNE: Yes, my marriage, I just wobble, even though I . . .

THEO: *"Begin thinking about what you would like your life to be. The reason you wobble is you have no picture of where to go. Start think-ing about what you would love . . . the possibilities for your life, and then it will give a vision to you. The reason you don't step forward is that you don't have the vision yet, and so you step back to what is known and familiar, yes?"*

ANNE: Yes.

THEO: *"So, begin envisioning and make that real in your vision for that new life. And you are very visual. You are good at that. So, see a new home. What does it look like? What does the furniture look like? What do the paintings look like? Is there much light in the windows, and what is the scenery like outside? Put yourself in that picture, and then you will become more comfortable in taking the steps forward."*

ANNE: I can do that.

THEO: *"Paint your picture with you in it."*

ANNE: Okay. Thank you.

THEO: *"You are complete?"*

ANNE: I think so unless there is anything else that I need to know.

THEO: *"You're on the path. There are times when you think you have not made any movement, but you have. You are not the woman we knew before. You are not the woman you knew before. There is greater strength still."*

ANNE: I can feel that.

THEO: *"Yes. And there is evidence in your life of those steps forward, of having your voice, the ability to say no, without anger. You have been able to do that."*

ANNE: I have been a lot better.

THEO: *"Yes, in saying, 'No, that is not my preference,' and it is accepted, isn't it?"*

ANNE: Yes.

THEO: *"See how far you have come."*

ANNE: Yes. Thank you.

THEO: *"And so it is."*

ANNE SHARES HER EXPERIENCE

The guidance I received from THEO has assisted me in a multitude of ways.

I have come to realize that my parents could never meet my needs in the way I wanted them to, and this encompasses childhood and adulthood. A huge revelation for me was when THEO said, "They could not do it for themselves." It now makes perfect sense to me that if they could never do it for themselves, how could they ever do it for me? A good part of the emotions behind this energy had to do with my dad. At one point in the conversation, THEO said, "You could never do anything right, could you?" I felt relief and thought, "WOW, it really was never my fault!" For years I carried outrage and anger within my being, and I do not regret it because I would have never known forgiveness and love if I never had this experience. I'm happy to say that I can let it go in this lifetime with my dad. This gives me so much gratitude. But leading up to this point of my life, I was wanting to be noticed and continuously proving myself to him. But how could he ever meet my needs when he never met his own? WOW! What an eyeopener that was for me!

The second "AHA" moment for me was when THEO said, "Because he couldn't see himself in that light, how could he see anybody else in that way?" When I read what THEO said in the transcription, I began to cry. This truth pierced my heart, and all the anger and outrage I have felt for my dad began to melt away. And for the first time, or maybe second time in my life, I understood what it truly means to forgive someone. Compassion is my new frontier, and this, in my eyes, is not a small task! At this moment, I feel love welling up in me, and I feel that this is one of the purposes for my being here, to learn this lesson.

I understand and know how I have carried this anger toward my husband as well, however I now know that it first started with my dad. It was never intentional. It was just what I knew, but now I know better. Because I know better, I can do better. I believe this to be quite an accomplishment.

I will end it with this: this little "girl" is growing up. She has experienced the love of self and worthiness. She knows she is stronger and wiser now, and she can be her own parent or "mother." Thank you, Mom and Dad, for breathing life into me and for THEO showing me how to love again.

MARCUS: **Speak to us about our relationship to our angels and non-physical guides, and share how the principles of Soul Integration create a deeper connection to them.**

THEO: *"So, most often, individuals do not ask for assistance. The legions of angels are waiting to be asked. They will not usurp your free will, but, oftentimes, the reason one does not ask is because there is resistance and a belief of being unworthy—not worthy to receive angelic presence."*

MARCUS: **How does loving ourselves affect our ability to manifest our dreams?**

THEO: *"Because there is no resistance."*

MARCUS: **It allows us to feel more deserving?**

THEO: *"You are all deserving."*

MARCUS: **It is our belief about it that matters.**

THEO: *"It is the belief that you deserve, and not from an arrogant or egocentric point of view or conceit or self-centered. Those are personality disorders. It is the truth of your divine being that is worthy of your dreams and desires being met."*

MARCUS: **Many people think the good thoughts, yet they do not think the law of attraction is working for them. The truth is that it is perfectly working all the time, isn't it?**

THEO: *"It is always working. It is like the law of electricity is always working. It exists. It existed before the conduits in which you must direct that electrical energy were brought forth. It was existing then. It is existing now. It is everywhere around you. The quantum field exists as well. And so, it is always working on your behalf. So, what are you thinking most about? You say, 'I wish, I want.' You have prayers for things that you wish to have. And then what is the second thought? For the second word or the second thought often has unbelievability and resistance. The resistance is not feeling worthy."*

MARCUS: Right. We speak about that as the "who-me?" fragment, meaning that we seem to think that others are more qualified or deserving somehow than we are. Some call it the impostor syndrome. But it could very well be for us if we just believed it, couldn't it?

THEO: *"It is, of course, for you. Why not you? You are a unique, divine being, in this human existence and human body. All is the same. One is not greater than the other, and you have a unique gift to give the world, each of you. It is miraculous that you are in the body, and you have what we call the soul note, a certain tonal quality. You have unique abilities and insights and visions that no one else has. Some might be similar but do not possess exactly what you have to give. It would be a very boring world if there was only one book because someone already did that, or one painting because someone already did that. Do you see what we mean? Each contribution is important to the whole."*

The "who me?" fragment often shows up as the "inner critic," which is a part of each of us, generated by beliefs about ourselves that are not true and seem to show up at the most inopportune times. Our good friend Mary Morrissey uses the analogy of a rocketship booster propelling us beyond our own gravitational pull instead of being pulled back into the old ways of believing. As you will see in this session with Elad, reminding ourselves of the evidence we have created in our lives—that we are not those limiting beliefs—will move you beyond this gravitational barrier, allowing you to enjoy each moment without the "inner critic" showing up.

THEO LIVE WITH ELAD

ELAD: Speaking of the relationship with the self, I don't know how to describe it, but there is an inner critic inside of me and it always shows up at the worst possible time. You are having a great time. You are on the rollercoaster. Everything is great. The wind is in your hair. Then, there is a small glitch. Something happens that you did not expect. Somebody said something to you that you did not want to hear, which should be okay, but you fall off. You dust off. You jump back in. But that inner critic is the one that pops up at that moment. "Do you really believe all this stuff?" "Why do you think you are special?" "Why do you think you will be successful?" It catches you in that moment that you say, like, "Wait a moment, that is not how I wanted it to happen. Of course, I didn't." So, how do you kill that inner critic?

THEO: "The inner critic is a fragmented aspect of yourself, of your soul. It is just stuck in a belief, like being frozen. You've heard us speak about being frozen in a moment in time where there was much judgment, and usually the judgment came from outside of yourself to begin with that informed, that part of self, 'Who do you think you are?'"

ELAD: Yes. When everything is clicking along.

THEO: "It is called an upper limit."

ELAD: Yes, that is exactly what it is.

THEO: "And so, how you change that is that you communicate with that part of self that is holding a belief that you are not that person, and how to do this is with a dialogue. You stop for the moment. That may be true then, but that was then. This is now. And you are the man, the person, that can achieve whatever you want to achieve. That is the human gravitational pull, just like the rocketship that is going off into space. The reason it has another booster is to go beyond the gravity. So, what you do when you get to that place where the gravitational moment of being pulled you back into the old way of being is ask 'What is your booster?' What is the thought that can move you beyond that gravitational pull out into space?"

ELAD: For me, it is all the evidence that I have seen it work.

THEO: "Yes . . . evidence. You have seen it work. That is just an untrue belief that wants to hold you back. There may be another piece to it. If you go beyond that, your life will change, and that is where the wobble comes from. Relationships will change as well because if you go beyond that, you will be different than all those that are on the other side of that gravity."

ELAD: Yes. And I have gone beyond that and have seen the other side. It is nice.

THEO: "Good. So, stay on your spaceship."

ELAD: Right—when this skeptic comes up.

THEO: "So when that 'Who do you think you are?' comes up, 'Who do I think I am? Accomplished. Moving through this to success. That is who I am.' Yes?"

ELAD: Yes.

THEO: "Claim that, because it is true."

ELAD: I usually do not take stock of what I have achieved. It is always on to the next thing.

THEO: "Yes. So, it is good to have a rearview mirror occasionally to see how far you have come. That is the evidence you need to build on to give you that booster through the gravity. That is, it—the evidence—because you are the man that is greatly accomplished."

ELAD: Yes. Thank you.

THEO: "So, it is."

ELAD SHARES HIS EXPERIENCE

For me, the concept that really sunk in from this THEO session is the idea of finding my "booster"—that thought or knowledge that you know to be fundamentally true. When random thoughts or beliefs show up to knock me off my center emotionally—usually out of fear or limiting beliefs—I can now use that fundamental touchstone to challenge them and see them for what they are—false premises built on fear and

lack. That is a process that can run all day without the awareness to change it. I am grateful for that awareness.

MARCUS: **When we talk about the law of attraction, are we talking
about the law of receptivity? Is that the same energy?**

THEO: *"It is similar, but the law of receptivity is just you knowing you are
worthy to receive it. It is exactly what we are talking about, knowing,
and believing. The reason many think it does not work is because
they do not believe in it and feel undeserving of it."*

MARCUS: **How would you define the quantum field, which is really what
you are talking about when you talk about the law of attraction?**

THEO: *"It is an energy field. Now those in physical science, quantum
physicists, have words for it. They can describe it, and they can give
equations, and they can do all of that. You would not understand
it either, just as we would want to speak of it as a vibrational frequency that permeates the atmosphere and everything around you
and is projected by you in thought. The quantum field is the 'out
of the blue' that you speak of. 'Out of the blue it happened. I don't
know how, but it showed up as if it just came from out of the blue.'
Where do you think the blue is? It is the quantum field."*

MARCUS: **Please share with us how loving the self leads us to be
nonattached to the good opinions of other people?**

THEO: *"Knowing that the opinions of others are their opinions and they
are viewing your situation, your circumstance, your choice by the
lenses that they see their life through. So, if they cannot envision
themselves in doing or being or having what you are discussing
that you wish, how can they possibly agree with you to have it for
yourself? It is all projection, isn't it?"*

MARCUS: **It is, so describe for us what it really means to establish
and maintain healthy boundaries.**

THEO: "That is a conundrum for most. How to establish healthy boundaries is to recognize that you are worthy of others treating you with respect, for you deserve to be treated like the master divine person that you are, and to treat others as the same. And those who do not respect you, do not deserve your time, energy, or presence. The word Namaste is used by many. 'I see the God in you. The God in me sees the God in you,' but that simply isn't true, is it? Many overstep their boundaries; many overstep with others. It is being mindful of that. Asking permission: 'Would you like to hear my opinion?' And if you are asking for opinions of others, be prepared that they are giving you their opinion. You do not have to follow it, and just know it is coming from inside of them and all their resistance and fragmentation. In other words, do not give your power away, and we are not talking about boundaries in a negative sense or being angry, for many reach a certain point. And then they get angry, and that holds boundaries. It does not have to get to that point. If someone is disrespecting you, you can say, 'That is not allowed. You are not allowed to speak to me in the manner that you have, in the tone and the words. I deserve to be treated with respect.' It is a simple conversation, truly it is, but you must live that as well. You cannot be one way for yourself and a different way for another."

MARCUS: So, if we have a negative thought or judgment about others, how do we shift that?

THEO: "It is mindfulness. Being mindful of your thoughts. If that is true, there are judgments of others. Follow that thread. Where is it coming from? What are you judging? Or is it just an observation? It is mindfulness—being aware of your thoughts, being aware of your actions."

MARCUS: That mindfulness assists us to view others with compassion and empathy. I would like you to talk about developing that vibration, or awareness, as our go-to way of being.

THEO: "You can observe a situation or a circumstance and not like what the personality is doing. You do not have to love the personality, and it does not excuse bad behavior when someone is acting out. It is appropriate to call inappropriate behavior inappropriate, but you can love the soul. And when you have compassion for yourself, you can have compassion for others. You all have the experience of that. You all have it within you. Now, there are some that do not or cannot show compassion for they do not know how. To expect them to do so is wasted energy, for they do not have the capacity for it, and that is not excusing bad behavior either. It is just what it is, and you can choose to participate with them or not."

MARCUS: **Please speak to the concept of soul age in the human experience.**

THEO: "There are different soul ages, and what that means is just specific to the human experience. Souls are eternal energy, but in the human experience, you have different soul ages because some are new to the experience of the human experience and some have had several lifetimes. So, a young soul is an infant soul, an adolescent soul. Then there is like the secondary education where there are more mature souls, and it is all human experience that gives one the ability to understand human life and emotions and experiences. Older souls have greater compassion and wisdom of the human experiences. Younger souls are usually of those personality disorders that are very self-absorbed.

MARCUS: **I would like you to talk about how not to take on other people's emotions for those who are empathetic.**

THEO: "All of you are empaths, so to speak. You are all ascension beings. Your bodies are your biggest receptors of energy. You have all intuitive gifts. There are those that are much more refined that use them as healing modalities and discernments, but know this, you have the ability to know what is yours and what is not, when you are absorbing energy from others. And so, you can allow it to pass through you, just like the wind passes through the limbs of a tree. The tree does not hold onto the wind. It notices it. It experiences it, and then lets it go. So, you too can allow that energy to pass through you and *not to hold it as your own, but it is informing you. So, what is the information you are receiving from it?"*

MARCUS: **How do we know what is ours and what is someone else's?**

THEO: *"How it feels. You all know. You have a truth barometer in you. If you ask the self, is this mine? You will know whose it is."*

MARCUS: **When we talk about developing and trusting our intuition, how important is meditation?**

THEO: *"Meditation allows you to center yourself and to focus. It allows an openness to receive and to hear, to calm the chattering mind to listen to the higher self for guidance that is there."*

MARCUS: **What do you say to those that try to meditate but they have constant thoughts running around in their minds?**

THEO: *"Do not resist them. Notice that they are there, and let them pass through and be dispersed."*

MARCUS: **Let's move on to the importance of forgiveness.**

THEO: *"You have recriminations of things that you have done or said that run repeatedly in your minds. It is done, but there is a necessity to communicate to another about it with the powerful words of 'I am sorry. If I knew then what I know now, I would react and act to you much differently.' But you can do the same for the self. 'I forgive myself, for whatever it is. If I knew then what I know now, I could have done things differently.' But now you know, and you will do things differently. It is all the part of the growth and expansion of awareness of consciousness."*

MARCUS: **Talk to us about how gratitude and self-love intersect.**

THEO: *"You can have gratitude for things and experiences, but when you love yourself that sense of gratitude is larger. It is a full awareness of the gifts that one has given the self."*

MARCUS: **It is our natural way of being, isn't it?**

THEO: *"It is, yes. It is an innate quality."*

MARCUS: **When we incarnate, we have a blueprint that we come in with that includes some life challenges necessary for our highest growth. How do we embrace the opportunities to find the** gift, the blessing, in each experience regardless of how difficult it might seem at the time?

THEO: "So you grow best when you are challenged, do you not? And so, the soul creates challenge to grow from, for a desired outcome from growth that is occurring in your life. So when you realize the soul draws unto itself perfectly situations, circumstances, and conditions to grow from, rather than the avoidance of them, there will be the embracing of them to find the gift, the learning, the jewel, that is there."

MARCUS: What if we are having a tough time finding that jewel?

THEO: "It is usually that you are stuck in the story of victimization. Victimized by situations and circumstances and conditions and blaming others for them. But when you recognize that everything is brought forth in your highest good, then it is an opportunity of expansion and growth, and recognition of the gift and the blessing. Oftentimes, when you are in it, you cannot see. It is after you have moved through the crisis or the condition that you can change the lens in which you see it and find the gift, the blessing. And it is not that you would want to experience it again, but you would recognize that it has been a part of your soul's growth, very instrumental in bringing you to your soul-centeredness."

MARCUS: As you say—"There are no victims, only volunteers."

THEO: "Yes. You choose to come into this human existence in this body. You choose the environment in which you were born. You choose your parents. You choose so that you may learn. The soul chooses perfectly. So it is that in each situation and circumstance, there is purpose. There is purpose in the learning therein. So, it is to trust the self. Life is happening through you and for you, not to you, so we advise not asking, 'Why is this happening to me?' It is happening for you, not to you, for it is the opportunity of growth and expansion that the challenges bring forth."

MARCUS: The soul's learning is eternal, isn't it?

THEO: "It is. Each lifetime gives you an opportunity of growth and expansion and experience, and the understanding of the human experience and compassion for it."

MARCUS: I think it is very empowering when you say that "No one ever makes us feel anything."

THEO: "You are responsible for your own emotional maturity, as is each person responsible for themselves."

MARCUS: Speak more to this, please.

THEO: "So, no one can do anything to you without your permission. So, if you are allowing bad behavior to continue, not being respected, you are not loving the self enough to say, 'It is not allowed.' It is happening for you to get the experience and understanding that you deserve respect and to speak out about it."

MARCUS: Talk about how loving the self can lead to better trusting of our intuition, leading to better decision-making and a deeper connection.

THEO: "So, it gives you evidence to trust your intuitive connection. You all have evidence in your lives where there was a strong knowing, a first impulse, that you did not follow. You let your conscious mind dictate the direction, only to find out you should have taken the first impulse, the first knowing. It was the correct one. So, it is understanding that it is to pay attention to your first impression, your first intuition."

MARCUS: Is the first time always right?

THEO: "Yes."

MARCUS: And then we talk ourselves out of it.

THEO: "Yes, the intellect wants to remain in control."

MARCUS: THEO, what have I not asked you on the topic of loving the self that you would like to share?

THEO: "We could reiterate everything that we have said. It is quite simple. It is releasing the patterns of thought about yourself that are simply untrue, and reframing, rewriting those words, and changing the beliefs that limit you, coming into that solid state of unconditional love."

CHAPTER FIVE

ROMANTIC LOVE

*Romantic relationships are a blessing in the
human experience that allow the heart to be
fulfilled, to become enlightened. Most seek to have
one, but most important is to become one."*

—THEO

AS YOU WILL READ SHORTLY THEO advises to write down all the values and characteristics you seek in a romantic partner. Put it on paper and be specific! When you have completed that, look at everything you wrote and ask yourself, "Am I that?" Do you possess all the values and characteristics that you desire in another? The process of attracting your partner is all energetic. Are you vibrating at the same frequency? (Are you a vibrational match?) What this means is: Are you on the same wavelength? Have you both "cleaned up your side of the street" emotionally? Are you both free from the old ways of thinking that if I fill up the woundedness in you, you will do the same for me? Or are you entering a relationship from a place of wholeness and desire, not neediness. The Dalai Lama sums this up well: "Remember that the best relationship is one in which your love for each other exceeds your need for each other."

Most people tend to underestimate the power of specificity when documenting what they are looking for in a partner. Several years ago, our daughter Jen, who lives in Los Angeles, began dating a young man named David. While we were in L.A. three months later, she asked if she could bring him to dinner. Well, what parents wouldn't love to meet the new boyfriend? As we were leaving our hotel room to meet them, Jen calls—clearly not happy with David—to say they were going to be late because he got the time wrong. We assured her it was no big deal and that we would see them when they got there. The four of us had a great time and towards the end of dinner, Jen pulls out a piece of paper with a list of all the characteristics she had written down that she was seeking in a partner—nice to know she had been listening to us—and pointed out that missing from her list was the word "punctual." We all had a good laugh, even David, but alas, that was the last time we saw him! The moral of this story, of course, is to be as specific as you possibly can when magnetizing "the one" into your life.

MARCUS: What is the first thing that we need to know about manifesting the love of our life?

THEO: "So you have a list of the things that are important to you. You have your core values and to find a match of your core values is to be aware of what they are, for a true match will not be unless your values are the same. But also, you have a list of things that are important to you of how to be treated with respect and how to be loved, and so, ask, 'Are you doing that for yourself?' For understand this, you must be the person you are seeking, to have those same qualities of you. Are you giving yourself that love?"

MARCUS: So, we need to love ourselves first if we are going to manifest the love of our life.

THEO: "Yes."

MARCUS: Tell us how you see the new paradigm in romantic relationships.

THEO: "The new pattern or the paradigm of relationship now is preferential. In the past, it has been out of need—that one would take care of you—and then you would take care of them, but it is from the inside out. Each and every one of you is capable of caring for yourself—providing a roof over your head and food, and all of the things that one may have needed assistance with in the past. The male going out and collecting food and the female cooking it, for an example. Each having their role, but in the need of the other, making them whole. But now you have the wholeness from within. So, it is not for need of someone fixing you or filling up that whole of expectations that have gone unmet, but meeting them for yourself, and then when a relationship is attracted, it is from that fullness, that wholeness of attracting another that has done the same, and that is a preferential choice, not a needy choice."

MARCUS: So, when you say, ". . . become the one we seek," what does that mean?

THEO: *"That is what we are talking about. You have a criterion of the things that you wish in another, in a mate, in a primary partnership. Do you have that in you? Are you a vibrational match to what you seek?"*

MARCUS: What does that mean: "vibrational match to the one we seek"?

THEO: *"It is alignment energetically, a likeness, if you would."*

MARCUS: So, are you saying that we only end up with a partner that is on the same vibrational frequency as ourselves?

THEO: *"Yes, because your beliefs are on the same frequency. If the expectations have gone unmet for you and for the other, there is a woundedness, and there has been an unconsciousness of the wound-edness in one, which leads to subconsciously seeking and being attracted to the woundedness in another with an unconscious or subconscious decision that if you could take care of their wounds, they will take care of yours, and it is an impossibility. Each is respon-sible for their own emotional maturity."*

MARCUS: I have heard you say in the past, write down all the things that you want in a mate.

THEO: *"Yes."*

MARCUS: Tell us how that works. Why is it so important?

THEO: *"Many know what they don't want. They are very certain of that, but it is important to know what you do want. What is of the great-est import? Most often, it goes along with your core values, the things that are important to you. If your core values for each of you are divergent, there is no vibrational match, and there is discord."*

MARCUS: How would you define soulmate?

THEO: *"You are on the same vibrational frequency. There are many soulmates, soul families. Many romanticize a soulmate, but it is not always romantic, although it can be. More importantly, you have the same core values; you have the same vibration; you are compatible."*

MARCUS: **Do we know prior to incarnating who our romantic partner is going to be?**

THEO: *"You know them, and you meet them along the way."*

MARCUS: **What is the relationship between destiny and free will regarding manifesting our partner?**

THEO: *"You are co-creators of your life. Understand this: the architect draws the pictures, a blueprint. The builder takes that blueprint, and first puts a foundation down and then builds the walls. But on the interior—the inner walls and rooms and places—things can be changed and reconstructed. That is what a life blueprint can do. There is a foundation; there is birth. You are co-creating by saying yes or no to opportunities, but the soul will always draw unto it opportunities to grow."*

MARCUS: **So, there is a blueprint of possibilities, but free will is also involved.**

THEO: *"Free will always wins out."*

MARCUS: **You have said before that angels never usurp our free will.**

THEO: *"That is correct. You are powerful divine beings. One is not greater than another, and you always have the ability to choose. And understand this: they are just choices. Aren't they? There is no right or wrong choice. You choose. You decide, obtain the growth . . . it is not static. There is a learning in every choice from which you receive the understanding and expansion."*

MARCUS: **How would you define twin flame?**

THEO: *"A like vibration—the masculine and feminine of one soul's energy."*

MARCUS: **So that is where I think it gets confusing—one soul's energy. But do we not have independent souls?**

THEO: *"You do. And it is so confusing that we wish you would not talk about it."*

MARCUS: **I understand that. I think we have a difficult time getting our heads around that one, even when we hear you explain it.**

THEO: *"And we find people looking for their twin flame or soulmate, and never quite finding the right one or thinking they have not, because* yes, the next one would be it because this could not possibly be the one, for it is challenging. But know, in any relationship, it is going to challenge you. If you live alone, you can always be right, but if you are in a relationship, you have feedback from another's perspective to give you a different perspective on your thoughts. That is the gift of a relationship, isn't it?"

MARCUS: It is. Talk to us about soul contracts.

THEO: "So groups incarnate together to support each other's growth, to make agreements to learn together and learn from. So, there are opportunities where you come together, and there are opportunities when that contract is complete, the learning has been done, then there is a separation of going a different way. You are living much longer now than ever before in human bodies, and so you can live several lifetimes in one body because of the longevity. So, of course, your soul contracts will become completed, and then you can meet and work with other souls by agreement."

MARCUS: Is there just one partner out there for us, or are there several that could be the one?

THEO: "Love is not limited. Unconditional love is never limiting. They are simply different expressions of that love, are they not? So, if one stated they had the love of their life and that person left their physical body, it would be an opportunity of more love to come. Yes?"

MARCUS: Yes, absolutely. How about karma in relationships. Is there such a thing as karma?

THEO: "We do not speak of karma in the way that most do. They speak of karma as a debt to be paid. It is not. It is only opportunities of growth and expansion."

MARCUS: Are there soul agreements about specific learnings we desire within a romantic relationship, and that is the purpose for coming together?

THEO: "Yes. There are certain paths to go down and people to meet and interact with and work to be done. It is a choosing, isn't it? And understand this, if you meet someone and have a reaction to them, *whether positive or negative, you can be assured that you have known them prior to that meeting."*

MARCUS: **Please speak to us about the soul's choice of sexuality in any given incarnation, the choice whether to be heterosexual, homosexual, or any other expression, and the learning therein.**

THEO: *"Everyone is both actually, but the preference of sexuality emerges in the human in their sensibilities and sensitivities and their preferences. But oftentimes, it is also biological, physical, or chemical. But why would one choose such a body? it is then asked, and each would be different in their own opportunity of growth and purpose."*

MARCUS: **Some would find it interesting that a soul would choose a transgender body, for instance, with the judgment and abuse they would likely experience.**

THEO: *"All soul choices are interesting. This is the judgment, and what we are talking about is persecution. When people do not understand, then they make it wrong. So, knowledge and awareness are extremely important for growth in the human experience."*

MARCUS: **To clarify, all choices are made by the soul for the purpose of the emotional learning therein?**

THEO: *"Yes, it is not that the learning is only for one. As you know, there are learnings for all that are involved with that individual, whatever the choices are. You are not islands unto yourselves in your own learnings."*

MARCUS: **You have said that we have all been male and female in previous incarnations. What is the masculine and feminine makeup of the soul, energetically?**

THEO: *"Neutral, ultimately. There is no gender-specific soul. That only occurs in physicality. But some would say in our group, there are those who have more feminine energy and others who are more masculine in their energetics and vibration, but that is just an assumption, an observation of what is experienced in the human experience."*

MARCUS: **To clarify, what you are speaking to is how we perceive** you, THEO, the 12 of you coming through as sometimes more masculine or feminine sounding or feeling.

THEO: "Yes, it is just an energy vibration, and communication and verbalization, vocabulary, but the energy is most predominantly felt and then one equates it to feminine and masculine because that is how you understand things in the human mind."

MARCUS: Anything more to say about that.

THEO: "Not really. It is very simple. It is the intellectual mind that wishes to make it more complex."

MARCUS: We experience that often in our community as people immediately seem to know each other, feelings of connection and love.

THEO: "Or it could be the opposite—contentious—but what did we say? You learn most when you are challenged. So oftentimes, your greatest teachers are those challenging soulmates."

MARCUS: What do you say to those who continue to repeat unhealthy patternings in romantic relationships?

THEO: "It is out of beliefs that one is not worthy of love. So, there is a recognition of what they think love might be, in a limited sense, and so, they keep looking for the same energy until they know differently. The patterns that keep repeating are out of the fragmentation of the soul."

MARCUS: What if we fear repeating unhealthy patterns to the point of shutting down?

THEO: "You will be very lonely. If you block yourself from relationship—and many do because of fear—you will say no to it. You slam the door, and that is a choice, isn't it? But we would invite you all to keep that door open, and most importantly, to keep the door open for the self. For when you move through and change those limiting beliefs, life is vastly different, and those patterns can shift and change."

MARCUS: Talk to us more about how your teachings of Soul Integration can assist us in manifesting joyous romantic relationships.

THEO: "How can you love another completely if you cannot love your-
self? It is an impossibility. Then you are seeking for expectations to
be met that are impossible for another to meet. Those are things
that must be met on the inner plane . . . the self-love. And if you do
not discover the love of self, you will continue to repeat the patterns
that dissatisfy you."

THEO's last answer speaks precisely to the guidance given to Legacy
in our next conversation. We often project an outer appearance of loving ourselves yet wonder why we are not receiving love in return. We
always attract that which reflects how we truly believe about ourselves,
that magnetic attraction THEO talks about. So use the feedback from
your outer world experience as an invitation to explore what aspect
of yourself doesn't feel loved and needs to be integrated. With this
awareness, a shift can occur immediately, as it did with Legacy.

Many breakthroughs and "Aha" moments also are accompanied
by an emotional release of tears, which is excellent! A lot of these
unloving beliefs have been holding us back from manifesting fulfilling romantic relationships for a long time, so we encourage you to
embrace the emotions and allow the tears to flow. You're going to feel
great afterwards, as Legacy did.

THEO LIVE WITH LEGACY

LEGACY: I have two questions, and I will start with the easy one first.

THEO: "We like easy ones."

LEGACY: What do I have to do to attract the relationship that I
want?

THEO: "There are many things that you think about that you don't want,
so that is what you are getting. So, start thinking about what you do
want. Get connected to what your values are and how you wish to
express them. Are you being kind to yourself? Are you loving yourself

enough? It is important to know that. That vibration is attractive, just like the other is. So, begin to communicate with those little ones inside of you that have beliefs that you are not worthy of that love."

LEGACY: I think I do have a lot of self-love, like I love myself a lot! I have been called a narcissist a couple of times because I love myself so much. It is just self-love. You should have the same self-appreciation as well for yourself. So, I do feel like I love myself a lot. But I am not receiving that vibration in return. I don't know what the missing piece is."

THEO: "That is what we are talking about. It is not external; it is internal. How old is this little one when she first felt abandoned?"

LEGACY: Five or six.

THEO: "Yes. This is the one that is holding the beliefs that she is not lovable enough, and so, she fights and becomes angry and makes sure she gets everything she wants. That is the narcissism you are thinking about. That is a different kind of love, isn't it?

LEGACY: Yes.

THEO: "So, the adult, you can love her and give to her and support her because that rigidity that she has is self-protection. She will not be abandoned. She can survive. She has made you the strong woman you are today. She is a fighter, but with that fight is fear that she may not survive. So, when you communicate with her, ask her what she needs. She does not have to be the soldier. Tell her that you love her and will not abandon her, and she can come into this new life and be fulfilled with you. She is not sure she knows what that means, or even what it looks like. It is not just material things. The solid state of unconditional love is not a feeling. It is a state of being—peace and aligned and comfortable in your skin. And when she reacts, it is a strong reaction. Let her know she does not have to be afraid. It is coming from fear—not being heard, not being seen. Let her know you are there, and you will not abandon her. And ask her if she wants to go into this new life that you are creating for each of you. What is her response?"

LEGACY: She says, yes! She is doing cartwheels. She wants to, for sure.

THEO: *"Good. Tell her now that you will come back and communicate with her, and she will always have a voice with you and that you love her. And ask her if it is all right to come back now, to this moment, and you will return and talk to her later."*

LEGACY: She says, "Yes."

THEO: *"Good. So, when you are ready come back to this moment . . . (Legacy begins to cry.) There it is. That is the love we are talking about."*

LEGACY: Absolutely.

THEO: *"You have opened the door now. Excellent."*

LEGACY SHARES HER EXPERIENCE

The guidance that I received from THEO has positively affected my life in so many ways. I want to first share the insight of being able to address, and talk to and heal, my inner child and how this has helped me with negative self-talk. I have forgiven myself and speak positive affirmations daily to my five-year-old self. This has assisted me in life to have more self-love and appreciation.

After leaving the retreat in Arizona and coming back to Los Angeles, I had a huge feeling of self-awareness in a whole new way. My perception of relationships had changed. I can't say that I magically came back and dating was a whiz. But I did gain a lot of insight into what was going wrong in my dating experiences. I know for a fact that I have been very lenient and understanding with my boundaries and non-negotiables and wondering why these relationships aren't working out. After several attempts of me trying to make things work with people that I knew early on were coming to the table with things that I do not want in my life, I knew this had to cease.

Secondly, I now realize that the five-year-old girl who

wants to be *loved, understood, heard, seen,* and most importantly, *accepted* by her partner, was making too many
accommodations for them out of a feeling of lack. Once I
gave myself permission to listen to my five-year-old self, I was
able to see and hold true to my boundaries, and dating has
become such an amazing experience since. These boundaries
are a direct reflection of now understanding the childhood
trauma, and to ignore her would only keep experiencing and
attracting trauma. I've ignored the needs of toddler Legacy
due to living in survivor mode. This newfound connection has
me feeling whole again.

Thirdly, I've started a book club with a group of amazing
women here in Los Angeles. When we all started this journey,
we were single, fed up, exhausted, and wanting to experience
pure joy and happiness with a life partner. Some are now hap-
pily dating, engaged, or married with children on the way. This
has been a great community to share, love, evolve, and grow
with as all of us have experienced something difficult in relationships that has been transformed into a joyous experience.
I am also live on Instagram discussing life in relation to the
book of the month and answering questions. I am also dating
someone right now, and it is night and day from what I was
attracting in the past. My dating experience has completely
transformed. I have been able to allow my five-year-old self to
have fun, to laugh, to be excited, to remain curious, and most
importantly be okay with speaking out, asking for help and
being vulnerable. It has been such an insightful experience.

MARCUS: What would you say to those who are in relationships that
feel stale and would like to be more spiritually connected, to
have that deeper resonance with each other?

THEO: "Love and attraction change as you mature with the relationship. First, there is lust. You are attracted physically and energetically, and that lasts for about two months or three months, a short time, and then it evolves into a different relationship. Either it stops because that was all that was there, or it deepens in the respect of one and another . . . and engagement. So, it is a deeper level of experience of love, and there is a continuum of a cycling that happens as you personally grow as well. Each person is growing and changing, and so there are ebbs and flows."

MARCUS: **What if our partner is not on the same spiritual path?**

THEO: "Then there is a choice, isn't there? There is always a choice. So, we are not telling anybody to do anything about that other than to be present in it and be communicative."

MARCUS: **THEO, how can we graciously invite our partners into our world, onto our path?**

THEO: "By sharing your experiences in your growth. But know, if they are asking for a sip of water, do not turn the hose on them fully and give them everything you know. They are not ready for it. So, in the asking, it is given. Too much information is overwhelming."

MARCUS: **What language would you give specifically to women who would love to invite the men in their lives onto their spiritual path?**

THEO: "Share the truth of your experience and the changes that you see in yourself. Many fear that they are going to be judged or ridiculed, and so they keep quiet. So first, speak to them that this is especially important to you, for oftentimes, you do not speak like that to each other. 'I need you to hear how important this is to me, and I would like to share it with you. Are you interested?'"

MARCUS: **What do you say to those who are having transformative spiritual and psychic experiences and want to share with their partners who are resistant because of fear?**

THEO: "The fear has to change in them. You cannot make it happen or *do it for them. There is a tendency to try to do it for them, but you cannot want more for someone than they want for themselves."*

MARCUS: **What if our partner just wants nothing to do with our spiritual path?**

THEO: *"Then, there is a choice to be made."*

MARCUS: **I guess we just figure out how important it is to us.**

THEO: *"Yes."*

MARCUS: **What advice do you have for people who are afraid of intimacy?**

THEO: *"Who inside is afraid of intimacy? It is one of the fragmented aspects of the soul that is afraid of intimacy who feels unsafe. Why do they feel unsafe? It is all part of the integration process. It seems redundant, but that is the key."*

MARCUS: **Many have been emotionally and physically abused creating a resistance to being intimate and vulnerable.**

THEO: *"So, you communicate with those parts of self that had those experiences. Again, history will not change, but your perception of it will. And the higher self, the whole self, the adult self, can support those little aspects that hold fear by loving them forward."*

MARCUS: **Speak more about "loving them forward."**

THEO: *"Bringing them forward into the present life. They are frozen in those moments, you see. That is where the fear comes from. So how do you defrost it? With love and encouragement . . . 'I will not abandon you. You did nothing wrong. You are lovable. I love you.'"*

MARCUS: **THEO, when you look at humanity today, do you see a balance between the masculine and feminine energies?**

THEO: *"It is coming into balance because each is equally important on this planet. There has been the patriarchal way of being, controlling, and there has been the desire for the feminine side that many speak of as goddess having the power. But when you recognize the masculine and the feminine are equal, you will recognize each bring into the human experience blessings and different qualities and strengths that should be celebrated."*

MARCUS: **How are we men doing?**

THEO: "Better."

MARCUS: **How so?**

THEO: "Because there is a different education that is happening. There is this wobble that has occurred, and men do not quite know how to act because they have been taught one way and now they're beginning to recognize that it is to be a different way. And so there is a little bit of confusion, but the women can assist that. They have always been in power, even though they think they haven't."

MARCUS: **I may have heard that before. And what can men do to assist women?**

THEO: "Communication. Speaking from the heart. The ability for vulnerability is your strength—that intimacy of which you are afraid. Most people think if they are intimate and share their most intimate thoughts that it will be used against them for that has been true historically, but one must step out into a new world, into a new way of being, and not be afraid of that. Soul-centeredness is the ability to step forward in that truth, and if another cannot accept it, it is not your issue. It is theirs."

MARCUS: **Please speak more about vulnerability. I know vulnerability is a great strength, yet many men and women still seem to perceive it as a weakness.**

THEO: "We see it as the same. And some women do still think of it as a weakness as well. That is what you have been taught; vulnerability means you are weak. It definitely does not in the context of what we speak. Those with greater strength allow their truth to be heard and known. They are not fearful that their truth and their beingness will be used against them in their ability to share their truest heart. That is what everyone wants to do but have thought they needed to protect that gentle heart, that softness inside."

MARCUS: So, how can we be vulnerable and yet stay in our personal power?

THEO: "If you tried, you would find it is power. Living in the truth of your being, your authenticity, gives support to that vulnerability, and you feel more powerful for you do not have to think about what you said yesterday because you would say the same thing again today. That is your truth. It is always said; it is always there within you. And that is the gift you give the world—that being, that light being, that divine master, courageous in that sharing."

MARCUS: In romantic relationships with a history of grudges, anger, or judgments, how can we shift that into a new way of being with love and compassion?

THEO: "If you know that you volunteered for the event, then you will not be so much in blame of another's fault. If you know you created it just as much as another, how would you change it? Yes?"

MARCUS: Yes, by taking responsibility.

THEO: "Yes, the ability to respond. It does not excuse bad behavior at all, but also it does not allow for you to continue to be victimized by it either. It allows you to step into that mastery and the ability to own your own boundaries and self-love."

MARCUS: What is the best way to communicate with our partners?

THEO: "Again, speak your truth. I feel loved when . . . and give the examples to your partner. And ask, 'When do you feel loved?' Get to know one another, and do not dance around. 'If I say this, then what will he do? Or what would she do?' Allow for that vulnerability and intimacy in the sharing. Communication is the key in all things."

MARCUS: Why is it so important that we communicate from our hearts instead of our heads?

THEO: "Yes, the heads calculate, don't they? The intellect is a problem-solver. So, working from the heart instead of the head is best. 'What would love do? How would love express?' For an example, if you are upset about an event or experience, own your own emotions . . . not *'you did this to me', but 'I felt devalued. My feelings were hurt when this happened.' Not 'you did it to me,' but it is acknowledging who you are in that vulnerability that we've been speaking about."*

MARCUS: In sharing our story, Sheila and I recounted some of the mystical experiences we had when we first got together. How can couples manifest these types of experiences?

THEO: *"You are opening the door as you do this integrative process to be more aware and connected to all that you are, all that you have been, all that you will be. You are aware of your multidimensionality, so it allows for opportunities to be experienced."*

MARCUS: In addition to belief and intention, is there anything you can share with us that we can practice.

THEO: *"Just make it welcome."*

MARCUS: How do we do that?

THEO: *"With intention and attention. When opportunities arise, pay attention to them. It is mindfulness. Yes?"*

MARCUS: Yes, it is. The last thing that I want to talk to you about on the topic of romantic relationships is sacred sexuality and Tantra.

THEO: *"Tantra is connection. It is being in the energy field of another with love—ultimately connecting. It is not just with words, but it is with energy and touch. The act of intercourse, of course, connects you, but with the connection we are speaking about, being in the energy field of another, being in that sacred space of divine essence with each other. That truth is a gift you give each other. And it does not have to be just in intercourse. It can be touching, being with another, listening, speaking, connection."*

MARCUS: THEO, what have I not asked you that we need to hear about romantic relationships?

THEO: *"It is not as complicated as you think. It is, first and foremost, to love the self and others as the self, and all will be well."*

We acknowledge that "to love the self and others as the self, and all will be well" sounds simple, but as with many things in life, it can be easier said than done. Therefore, we devoted the previous chapters to this topic to lay the foundation for being the vibrational match to the romantic relationship we desire. We love THEO's statement in their session with P.K. that what many consider "love at first sight" is really "love at first vibrational match." What if it's not about looking or seeking but rather attracting and magnetizing? This is part of THEO's message to P.K.

Many of us also tend to take responsibility for other's emotions, worrying about hurting their feelings if things don't work out, even when we have honorable intentions. THEO reminds us that we are all volunteers in these interactions, that there are no victims, and each will get the gift of the lessons learned as we move forward. This is also the first mention of THEO's teachings that if we believe it possible and make good choices, we can live healthfully to140 years in this lifetime and encourage us to trust in the perfection of the timing.

THEO LIVE WITH P.K.

P.K.: When we meet the one, you have said that we will know it. What are the signs that I should look for when I meet that person? Acceptance, connection, chemistry, wholeness, and as you said, a feeling of self-love? Beyond all of this, is there anything else I should look for?

THEO: "It is an energetic attraction, isn't it? Some of it has to do with visual attractiveness and then an energetic attractiveness, and then as you begin to speak, there is a compatibility in your thinking, yes?"

P.K.: Is there any way to meet that person? We will know after spending some time together that we are compatible. Is there any way to find out without wasting her time or emotions?

THEO: "Wasting time. Is that true?"

P.K.: I do not want to waste her time if we are not compatible.

THEO: "You don't want to waste her time, how generous of you. The truth is that you do not want to waste your time either. Correct?"

P.K.: Yes. I am concerned that she will be more hurt if I leave, or if something happens, or even if she leaves.

THEO: "Understand this: you are both there by choice. Each of you is responsible for your own emotional maturity. If there is not an intention of harm or hurt to another, then you are not responsible for hurting them. How another reacts in that situation is their responsibility in their ability to respond to life. However, know that you have come together to do this dance of interaction, but when you meet the one that many speak about, or the one you are to be with or spend time with, it is not a waste of time You are both testing yourselves in how to be in relationship with the self and with another. It is a gift you are giving each other. But for the one you are to be with in a committed way, there will be no doubt. There will be a strong knowing immediately. Some talk about it as love at first sight, but we would say more, it is love at first vibrational matching. But what you are talking about is expectation, the expectation that one has of another to fulfill them. And, in the past, the paradigm of relationship of need has been an individual subconsciously finding the woundedness in the other with the expectation that they would fulfill the woundedness in you, so that 'I will take care of you and you will take care of me' . . . a quid pro quo—we hear that word a lot these days—but that is what it is, isn't it?"

P.K.: It is. What I am looking for is what a lot of people refer to as a soulmate, you know, that kind of connection. So, are there any signs for that?

THEO: "Yes. It is all those attractions. It is a vibrational noticing. The new paradigm is preferential, not needy, for as we have spoken of this, there is an awareness of that neediness that came before. There has been a learning about that and the personal growth that has been done within it. So, the desire for a preferential relationship is an awareness that you have in you that which will attract that *independence and that awareness in another, because you have grown. And you know more now from that personal growth that has occurred."*

P.K.: So that is what is called a soul connection?

THEO: *"Yes, it is a vibrational connection. Of all the people that you meet in a lifetime, and there are thousands, how many are you truly attracted to? Not that many. Correct?"*

P.K.: Correct. Maybe that is why I am having a hard time connecting with people. It seems hard.

THEO: *"Let's change that. Let's change the words 'it is hard' to 'it is easy.' 'I can do this with ease and grace.' 'I am the man who is open and receptive to an unconditional loving relationship now.'"*

P.K.: I tried but somehow, I seem to repel them. I connect, and then it is gone.

THEO: *"It is feedback. It is just feedback. It is not the right person vibrationally.*

P.K.: Yes, that is what happens.

THEO: *"It is just not a match, but it is good to know, isn't it? It is better to know when it is not a match than to try to make it a match and then find out later it is not."*

P.K.: But how long do I have to do that to find a match?

THEO: *"It will find you. Live your life. Be open to the friendships that come. We see it is not long off, but you are making it harder than you need to. So, when you think in terms of the relationship that you want, the qualities in the person that you want, what you can ask the self is 'Am I that?' 'Do I give that to myself?' 'Am I that person with those qualities on the inner?' They are your core values as well."*

P.K.: Yes. That is what I am looking for. I have my core values, but it does not match people I have met so far.

THEO: *"So far . . . Up until now. Up until now does not mean you are not going to, but your mind goes to time. I don't have much time left—I better find somebody."*

P.K.: We are all mortal.

THEO: "If you believed you could live to 140, that would change your mind, wouldn't it? So, you have that time. Nobody knows when they are going to leave the planet initially. You have this moment, this now. But be open to all relationships and conversations and communications, without the 'I have to do it now,' because that creates resistance, a barrier, to time and timing. But know when you meet, you will realize it could not have been before that moment for either one of you because of the life's situations and circumstances you both have had and the inner growth that was necessary for you to come together."

P.K. SHARES HIS EXPERIENCE

My weekend turned out to be a miraculous experience with THEO. It opened my mind to the most important relationship of all—the core relationship with me. Since that weekend, I started focusing on my self-care, and I saw the better version of myself start to appear slowly. I began by doing yoga, meditation, dancing, massages, and lots of other healthful activities, including working out and walking. I am now able to sleep better without any alcohol or drugs. I connect with people better on a business and personal level. I received almost everything I wanted, and there is lot more to come because I can feel it coming. One day soon, I will meet someone who will love me the way I am going to love her. Then I will say that the first chapter of my journey into The Art of Relationship is complete. This is important to me because now that I am loving myself, I know I will be ready for love when she comes into my life.

CHAPTER SIX

HONORABLE
SEPARATION

"Releasing relationships in an honorable way,
understanding that it can be done lovingly. It
is a gift you give to yourself and others."

—*THEO*

YOU MAY HAVE HEARD the old saying that relationships are for a reason, a season, or a lifetime. Knowing which is which can save you a lot of heartache and emotional turmoil, whether it be a relationship with a romantic partner, friend, family member, business associate, or employer. Many relationships simply run their course, and there is never any shame in ending them. Recognizing and being grateful for the gifts, the blessings, and the opportunities of growth will assist you to end them honorably. When you know that you, your soul, created the relationship in the first place, and that as THEO says there are no victims just volunteers, you will not feel the need to blame or feel victimized when any relationship ends. You may ask, "But what if I was betrayed?" which is a great question that we will discuss in the next chapter.

Imagine all your relationships as a mobile, like a mobile you would see hanging over a baby's bed. As you grow and expand psychically and spiritually and take steps toward manifesting your dreams and desires, you may find some in your life not supportive of your path. They may want to place upon you the limitations they hold for themselves. The mobile becomes unbalanced. New relationships of all kinds are now being formed out of preference, not need, and there is a magnetic component to each where you feel the energetic resonance of someone vibrating at a similar frequency as you, attracting to you those of like mind, heart, and energy.

One of our favorite Buddhist quotes is: "One of the greatest sources of all pain and suffering is resistance to what is." Sounds simple, right? But the reality is that it is much easier said than done for most people. An example of the freedom that can be felt from non-resistance can be found in a story shared by a friend of ours who was engaged in legal proceedings [which THEO will typically suggest you avoid whenever possible as you evaluate the energetic drain of most lawsuits] with a soon-to-be ex-husband. At the time, she thought that her powers of persuasion and reason were so strong that she could somehow convince him to think in a way that would be "more reasonable." Fortunately, she had a moment of clarity—an "aha moment"—when she realized that there was absolutely nothing she could say or do that was going to change his thinking, behavior, or intentions, and she simply stopped resisting, thus leading to a satisfactory outcome. She reported feeling a powerful sense of liberation, a big exhalation, because of this realization.

If you find yourself going through a separation, personal or professional, remember that the energy of the dissolution of one relationship will carry over to the beginning of the next. Unresolved emotional issues will remain, leading to the repetition of old, unhealthy relationship patterns. This is another example of why the soul integration process can be so powerful.

MARCUS: How do you define honorable separation?

THEO: "It is a new way of separating from relationships, friendships, committed relationships. When the contract is done, what is important is to remember the love. The old way of separation has been for individuals to become angry and judgmental and to point out 'You did this to me,' or you did that to me,' to feel comfortable in completing it. You do not have to be in that place. You can honor what each has given to the relationship, the gifts that have been given—not pointing out all the bad things, all the expectations that have gone unmet, for many of those are the responsibility of the self; expectations, fantasy of self, of what could have been, which another cannot fulfill for you anyway. Expectations unvoiced can never be met. So, it is to recognize the goodness that has been brought, and remember the love, for you loved this person or you would not have been together. So, remember that. You are just going different ways, different paths of growth. It is not right or wrong, good, or bad. It is what is the soul's direction."

MARCUS: **What determines when a contract ends?**

THEO: "Each person knows when the contract is complete, when it is not a vibrational match. There is not the compatibility. There is not the ability to communicate. You are missing communication. You are not speaking the same as you have in the past. The vibration will tell you."

MARCUS: **Tell us about the new paradigm in ending relationships consciously, honorably.**

THEO: "We spoke a bit about that. The old ways have been to express anger and the projection of expectations that went unmet. The victimization of 'You did this or you did not do that,' for then anger motivates the individual to say, 'It is all right; I do not have to be sad to leave this relationship because of all these negative things.' It is important to understand there are necessary endings in life that must be grieved, and the sadness you are trying not to feel is the grieving of what could have been. That is what grief does. Expectations unmet. Things undone possibly that one desired or imagined would happen. So, it is not to avoid feelings or emotions. To embrace them allows for the release to get to the place of gratitude for what has been achieved, what has been learned—the gifts and the blessings."

MARCUS: **We feel like we need to get angry and blame the other to justify our actions, don't we?**

THEO: "Yes, uncomfortable feelings. Anger is more acceptable, isn't it?"

MARCUS: **It is, but it does not feel good blaming another.**

THEO: "Sometimes it feels good for a moment, but the heart, the soul, knows the truth of it . . . that each one is there by choice—volunteers."

MARCUS: **How do we finally get to that point of knowing it is time to leave, without doubt?**

THEO: "You all know when there is a completion, but oftentimes, you stay too long at the party—making the other even more wrong. In *doing so, you are not being authentic and in your truth for fear that you are going to hurt someone's feelings. Understand this: each person is responsible for their own emotional maturity, and if you think that you have all the power and you are going to hurt them beyond repair, it is a bit arrogant, isn't it? Know that the dance of relationship is an opportunity for both. You are not dancing alone."*

MARCUS: Can you give us some insights as to how to separate with compassion and love?

THEO: "By telling the truth. Most often, that is what betrayal feels like if someone does not tell the truth, and that is what you are trying to avoid. There is no reason for you to not tell the truth and for making another wrong, when the truth is that you are just complete in the relationship and moving in another direction. It does not mean you are going to be with another in that time, but it can mean that you have grown in different ways, are on different paths. And so, telling the truth about that is more important than just being angry and letting the other wonder what had happened. But the fear of abandonment on your part can dictate how you end relationships."

MARCUS: Speak more to the fear of abandonment.

THEO: "So if that is permeating your thinking process or your feeling process, it is to understand that it then colors everything. That is why you do not want to leave or be the bad person, to step out and hurt someone's feelings. The greater feeling is that you may be abandoning them, and they will be greatly hurt. And that is a projection of your own feeling."

MARCUS: How do we not take on that fear of hurting their feelings?

THEO: "They are going to feel whatever they are going to feel. You are not responsible for that. The sooner each person releases responsibility for another's feelings, the sooner you can let go with compassion. We are speaking about kindly speaking the truth—the truth will out, but if the truth is spoken with anger and then there are grievances added on, that is inappropriate."

MARCUS: **What do you mean when you speak of "weeding the garden"?**

THEO: *"Weeding of the garden, meaning you have all these relationships in your life that serve you until they do not, until you are all completing and going on your paths, that you have given all you can give, and you are feeling a disconnect, energetically. So that allows for the change to come, the weeding of the garden, as many weed gardens. You just make a clean path between the flowers or the vegetables, or whatever your garden grows, but if the growth is completed, there is the necessity of weeding out that which is complete."*

MARCUS: **It makes room for the flowers.**

THEO: *"It makes room for new growth."*

MARCUS: **Tell us about the relationship mobile.**

THEO: *"It is true in family or work relationships where there is a common goal or friendships, like a child's mobile in their room, each piece hanging in balance to another at different links, if you would. What happens when you take one of the pieces off, the balance is askew, isn't it? Well, that is true in relationships, in community, and in family. And what occurs is there needs to be an adjustment, a new adjustment for those left in that mobile . . . and some will not like that."*

MARCUS: **What is the best way to respond to the people in our lives who do not support our spiritual path?**

THEO: *"Yes, this part of the path can be uncomfortable or confusing. But is that not true in anything? You become educated, and it may not be in alignment to those as well when you are a part of the mobile. Anytime there is growth and change, there is change amongst relationships—either it is compatible and each is going with that change, or it is not. But it is not right or wrong, good or bad, or that people are good or bad. It is just an energy shift. When one shifts their vibrational frequency and it is not in alignment to another's, it does not mean you are right and they are wrong. It is just change, and what you can always count on in life is change. And the more you flow with change and not resist it, the easier life is."*

MARCUS: I believe it was Jim Rohn who I first heard say that we become the five people we hang out with the most. Do you agree with that?

THEO: "In any relationship, there is a vibrational match until there is not, and what creates that is growth, personal growth and expansion, and becoming more aware of the authentic self. Who you really are. What your desires are. What your learning is to be. Your soul draws unto you perfectly, and so in that process, your vibration and your frequency changes. It is like listening to your radio. There are certain megahertz that align to certain stations, you call it, but if your dial is not set perfectly on that megahertz for clear communication, there is static, and it is uncomfortable. You cannot listen to it. The words are spotty. There is a hissing sound until you dial to a perfect vibrational match. That is what happens in relationships. When you are not matched any longer, there is static."

MARCUS: What would you suggest when the person we are separating from decides to stay in an unconscious pattern of blame and anger?

THEO: "That is a judgment."

MARCUS: Right, it sounds a little judgmental, doesn't it?

THEO: "Yes."

MARCUS: So, help me with that one.

THEO: "They are just choosing to be at a particular frequency. It is all choice. Everything you do is a decision and a choice that you are making, and if you are not making a decision, indecision is a decision in and of itself. You are allowing life to happen to you unconsciously, not directing the energy and the outcomes you desire. Life is happening through you and for you, not to you. No one is a victim. You all volunteered to be on this planet, to be in these bodies, and to be in life itself. You create the life you wish to live."

MARCUS: Why do we stay in indecision when we know in our heart it is time to leave?

THEO: "One would ask the self, 'Who are you protecting?' You are not *protecting the other person. You are protecting yourself from feeling uncomfortable, to have the discussion, or to speak, afraid of judgment from another."*

MARCUS: **When you say indecision is a decision unto itself, speak more to that.**

THEO: *"We will give you an example. If you decide—and it is a decision, and you can align with this type of decision because you have all done it—to stay in bed with the covers over your head. What is the result in that decision? You have stayed in bed with the covers over your head. That is the result, isn't it? If you stay in a relationship because you are afraid to speak your truth, that is a decision, and the decision that benefits you ultimately from having uncomfortable feelings that you are trying to avoid."*

MARCUS: **And it's always in their highest good to just tell the truth, to face those uncomfortable feelings.**

THEO: *"If you complete and release them, of course, they have an opportunity to shift and change and grow in the direction they want or choose to, but if you stay out of resistance to feeling uncomfortable, that is not good for the other person at all, for the energy is still there in its static position."*

To stay in an unfulfilling relationship out of a resistance to feeling uncomfortable feelings may be the most common reason for remaining. Our friend Dr. Joan Rosenberg, in her excellent book, *90 Seconds to a Life You Love*, identifies the eight most common unpleasant emotions that we avoid as sadness, shame, helplessness, anger, embarrassment, disappointment, frustration, and vulnerability. Dr. Rosenberg explains that "most people believe that shutting down unpleasant emotions they're feeling will lead to a greater sense of control and emotional strength; instead, such shutting down tends to leave you feeling more vulnerable, helpless, and out of control. What most often blocks people from success and feeling capable in life is the inability to experience, move through, and handle these eight unpleasant feelings. Knowing how to deal with intense, overwhelming, or uncomfortable feelings is essential to building confidence, emotional strength, and resilience. Yet when we distract or disconnect from these feelings, we move away from confidence, health, and our desired pursuits, ultimately undermining our ability to fully realize our ambitions." She also states that when we do allow ourselves to feel these unpleasant emotions, they usually last only 90 seconds.

In this session, Anne has an "Aha" moment as THEO identifies how the transference of unmet expectations from her mother to her husband illuminated certain patterns and beliefs being repeated that led to anger and her fear of moving forward. Anne also has the awareness that she can now move out of a relationship that was originally entered into out of need, into the new paradigm of creating a relationship from preference and remembering the good things about the partner she is leaving.

THEO LIVE WITH ANNE

ANNE: What is holding me back from holding boundaries with my husband moving forward?

THEO: *"You have been learning how to do some of it since we last spoke, haven't you?"*

ANNE: Yes.

THEO: *"So, you are learning. You have taken some baby steps forward in that, but it is all about survival. For in that time of the two of you coming together, it was out of need, and if you did not agree with him, the thought was 'What if he would leave, and how would I survive?' But you are very accomplished in your own self. And the truth of it is you would survive, but it is just a belief that is held from that little girl inside of you, of which you are familiar. So, what would you say to her?"*

ANNE: I would tell her that she is safe, that she can handle this, and that everything is going to be okay.

THEO: "He has convinced you that it won't be, hasn't he?"

ANNE: He has.

THEO: "Over many years."

ANNE: Right.

THEO: "'What would you do without me?'"

ANNE: Basically yes, that is the impression.

THEO: "And you believed it."

ANNE: Yes.

THEO: "So, talk to those parts of yourself that hold that belief."

ANNE: Okay.

THEO: "Speak to her of that, and believe in yourself. That is what is important."

ANNE: Yes. I struggle with that, believing in myself, but I am much better at it.

THEO: "You are much better at it. You have done many things to prove to yourself that you are accomplished, which is good. Yes?"

ANNE: Yes.

THEO: "How much like your mother is he?"

ANNE: Yeah! Oh wow! 100%.

THEO: "So that is where this began."

ANNE: Yes, I can see that, and that is why it has been hard to pull away, I guess.

THEO: "That little girl is still seeking the mother's love, and only if she would do everything asked, would she be accepted."

ANNE: Meaning my mother or me?

THEO: "Between you and your mother, but you then transferred it to your husband."

ANNE: Right.

THEO: "And in this relationship, there were expectations that went unmet for you from your mother that were transferred to him."

ANNE: Okay, I see.

THEO: *"That was impossible for him to meet, which created anger at him. Yes?"*

ANNE: Yes, there is a lot of anger there.

THEO: *"Yes. But he could not meet those expectations. Only you can meet those needs for her on the inner. You are the best mother for this little girl. So, let her know that you love her and will not abandon her, and you are going to have a new life. It is emerging as we speak. You are taking steps for that occurrence and becoming stronger."*

ANNE: Is it good that I am living at the lake right now?

THEO: *"Yes, isn't it?"*

ANNE: Yes, I think it is. I feel like it has strengthened me somehow, but I find that I am scared being alone because it is kind of out in a remote area.

THEO: *"You are challenging yourself."*

ANNE: Yes.

THEO: *"You will be just fine. And if you can handle being out in a remote area that is a bit frightening to be alone in, you will notice that you will become more content with it."*

ANNE: I already kind of feel that happening.

THEO: *"Yes, you have been there for a bit of time."*

ANNE: Yes.

THEO: *"Good, that will give you the confidence to take those steps going forward."*

ANNE: Okay, I see that happening. There are a lot of tears here that I feel like I need to . . .

THEO: *"It is grief. Yes?"*

ANNE: Yes.

THEO: *"The grieving of what could have been, but there is a lot of goodness there as well, yes?"*

ANNE: Yes.

THEO: *"And that is good to remember*

ANNE: I know.

THEO: "You have just outgrown each other, yes?"

ANNE: Yes.

THEO: "But remembering the love and what attracted you is important as well. That is a gift. You do not want to lose that."

ANNE: Right. It has been 35 years, but I am ready. I am ready.

THEO: "For a new life to be lived. A new book to be written of life."

ANNE: Yes. A real book or just a book of my journey?

THEO: "A real book."

ANNE: Yes, that is what I am feeling.

THEO: "Yes. Good."

ANNE: I am starting it soon. I am taking a course.

THEO: "So, you have already begun."

ANNE: Yes.

THEO: "Acknowledge those steps that have been taken."

ANNE: Okay.

THEO: "Do not be harsh with the self that you have not done it yet."

ANNE: All right.

THEO: "You were a bit afraid to speak to us about this."

ANNE: Yes, I was. I was afraid to bring it up.

THEO: "Because it takes as long as it takes. It is a process, and there is no judgment to the choices of life, because there are those steps moving forward. And you are taking them for the self."

ANNE: I feel a little trepidation, though. I am scared to really step out, but you say it takes steps, baby steps.

THEO: "Yes. It is feeling the fear and doing it anyway, and that is what you have been doing."

ANNE: Right.

THEO: "And it was an enormous state of fear."

ANNE: Correct. It was huge.

THEO: "So have gratitude for yourself for how far you have come. Look how far you have come."

ANNE: I have, thank you. Thank you for reminding me of that.

THEO: "There is a tendency not to see it. You are always thinking about *the future and not recognizing the large steps you have taken to get to this point. It is a life that you are living, a long life, and this is just a part of it along the journey."*

ANNE: Thank you, THEO. Thank you so much. I love you.

ANNE SHARES HER EXPERIENCE

I had the opportunity to be part of a weekend workshop called "The Art of Relationship" and had an authentic conversation with THEO regarding my marriage. It has been one year since THEO and I conversed on this subject, and I share here how it has unfolded for me. I will begin with this statement that THEO said to me:

"For in that time of the two of you coming together, it was out of need, and if you did not agree with him the thought was 'What if he would leave, and how would I survive?'"

This phrase caught me off guard, and I believe that it did because it rang so true for me. I knew when I married him that I was "needy," but now I have grown in unbelievable ways. I have become authentic with others and, most importantly, with myself. I have learned to turn within to find my answers. Most of my married life, I depended on his approval and insight, while negating my own knowing, which caused anger and bitterness. The good news now is I know this was happening, and I have started to turn the lens within myself instead of blaming him. I was afraid of his disapproval. I began to speak up about my feelings even with the fear of rejection or abandonment. This was very liberating for me, and my heart started to heal from the heartbreak. I am breaking from this need and realizing I do not have to settle because I am now feeling more empowered than I have ever been. I also can make decisions on my own because I now know that I am capable and can trust myself.

THEO also said that "my husband is like my mother, and

that little girl is still seeking the mother's love and expectations that went unmet for you from her that were transferred to him." I used to look at this with a view of co-dependency, looking for love and approval from him, thinking that he knew what was best for me. I have grown in bountiful ways, such as holding boundaries with him because I now know that I can stand on my own two feet without getting permission from him. Now I understand why I harbored anger, stemming from the "expectations that went unmet." As THEO said, "He could never meet my needs, that I was the only one who could do that." I continue to learn every day to show love, compassion, and deservability towards this child within me that felt abandoned. I continue to grieve the loss of moving on from this relationship with my husband as it is all I have known, but now I know better. We have outgrown each other. It is like a glove that no longer fits. My heart speaks to me through my knowing. I feel good about my decision, and my body feels good too because my body knows truth!

MARCUS: Let's talk about how the energy of completing one relationship affects the energy of the beginning of the next one.

THEO: *"It is not clean. What we mean by that is you are still carrying forward the energy of the old that is unresolved. So there is a projection of that unresolved energy, isn't there?"*

MARCUS: Right, so let's flip that and talk about how having an honorable separation positively affects the next relationship.

THEO: *"You are not carrying forward all of those expectations that have been unmet, for you are fully realizing that it must come from the inner to the outer and not from the outside to the inside."*

MARCUS: One of the most difficult relationships to separate from is our birth family.

THEO: "It can be a vibrational mismatch to them as well. Understand, the soul chooses to be in a family, in a particular community or environment, and a family is community. But a soul can choose the mother only, or the father only, or a sibling only, to be a part of that group; for whatever reason, the soul desires the interactions there. Understand this: your nuclear family, your birth family, your genetic family, is not always your soul family. They are there, as you are, as a teacher and a student, each of you, and for whatever energy is there that the soul is desirous of experiencing to grow from."

MARCUS: Many ask, "How in the world did I end up in this family?" and feel like the black sheep of the family.

THEO: "We think black sheep are very beautiful."

MARCUS: Absolutely.

THEO: "So that just means when one speaks of that, they do not feel like they fit in. But who is your greatest teacher? Who challenges you the most in those relationships? Who are you most aligned with? You do not have to align with everybody just because you are genetically connected. The vibrational connection is soul to soul."

MARCUS: We seem to have adopted the belief that we are somehow obligated to our birth family. Speak to us about obligation. And what if the things we feel obligated to do not bring us joy?

THEO: "That is different. Obligation does not have to be a negative. It can be a choice, to assist those whom you care about and love. You feel obligated to do it, but who is benefitting? You are. Yes, the residual effect is that you are assisting them, but you are doing it out of love, a choice. The obligation you are speaking of is you are doing something that is not a choice. That you feel the reason to be loved or liked, or to be part of this group, you must do something for another that you do not want to do. And so, most often, you do it begrudgingly because the energy of anger and discontent is projected upon whatever you are doing, and so there is this divisiveness, this energy that is not coherent."

MARCUS: We do it to be loved, don't we?

THEO: "Most often. Pay attention to your intent behind any action. What do you expect to receive from it when you are doing something for another? There is always an expectation: 'I will do this for you, and I will get this from that action,' and most often it is desiring love or acceptance."

MARCUS: So, the question becomes: Are we doing it out of love? Or are we doing it to be loved?

THEO: "Mindfulness. Awareness. Most people, until they know they have power, are asleep. They do things by rote. They are not aware of why they are doing them; they just do them and wonder why they are feeling the way that they are feeling. They never ask the inner questions: 'Where is this coming from? What part of me is feeling discontent?' If you could see yourselves as we see you, there would be no discontent. You would be in a soul-centered place. That divine essence. But the human experience gives you discontent. You are learning emotions through your human experience and through your human body, your earth suit that navigates this planet that gives you the experiences you have come here to learn—emotions. Imagine this . . . how exquisite it is to have this physical body where you can feel viscerally all the things we are talking about. Without a body, you could not. You would not have these exquisite experiences to touch and be touched. It is an exquisite opportunity, a rich opportunity, of soul growth."

MARCUS: What is the difference between joy and happiness?

THEO: "Joy is a contented feeling. You feel happy when someone holds you. You feel happy when you buy a new thing, a new material thing, that you have wanted. You are happy. But joy is something that is in every cell of your body. It is that vibration of soul-centeredness. It is consistent energy. One can feel joy and that contentment and soul-centeredness no matter what is happening in their outer world circumstance. Understand this, the earth plane gives you challenges— that is how you grow best—but it is like the eye of the hurricane. The eye of the hurricane is calm and centered. It matters not how fast *the winds are circling around the eye. It remains calm, and when debris is flying by, it is still calm. That is what we are talking about in the soul-centeredness place. Whatever challenge is there that will pass, growth will happen, new opportunities of growth will come—not as severe as the last because you have found that centered in soul-ness and you are not creating chaos continuously, as most do until they find their soul center."*

MARCUS: **Talk to us about guilt.**

THEO: *"It is a gift you give yourself continuously, isn't it?"*

MARCUS: **The gift that keeps on giving.**

THEO: *"Yes. And what are you getting from it? That is what you must ask yourself. For every action, there is an equal reaction. So, if you are feeling guilty, what is the reward in that? The rumination of what has happened in the past keeps you from being in the present. You must ask yourself if you are feeling guilty. Is there something or someone you need to apologize to and for? The greatest gift you give another is to say, 'I'm sorry' and mean it. 'If I knew then what I know now, I would have acted very differently.' That is what most find at the end of their lives when they leave their physical structure; where they may have come up short in their relationships."*

MARCUS: **So, guilt can be a trigger for asking more highly calibrated questions?**

THEO: *"It can, yes. What would you have done differently in that circumstance? It is a growth question, isn't it? And what if you shared that with another—that you are feeling guilty about. What if you shared that truth with another and what it would do for them? It is a loving thing to do, isn't it?*

MARCUS: **Absolutely.**

THEO: *"What would love do?"*

MARCUS: **Right. Let's talk about friendships, and loyalty, particularly with old friends with whom we are no longer feeling resonant.**

THEO: *"That is a very tricky question, isn't it?"*

MARCUS: **It is.**

THEO: "Yes. Loyalty, it is truth, isn't it?"

MARCUS: Yes.

THEO: "So, you are loyal to a friend or to someone whom you know. It does not mean you have to stay together."

MARCUS: An old friend, or an employer, neither one is working, but we still feel loyal. Isn't loyalty earned?

THEO: "Yes. It is not freely given. But understand this, things change. You are loyal to an employer, and the reason is that they provided you with a job. And you will earn an income, and so you feel beholding to them. That is different than loyalty to a friendship. But anytime there is a change and a release of relationship, it can be done elegantly, and we do not use that word lightly. It can be messy, or it can be elegant. Which do you choose?"

MARCUS: Let's talk about the elegant route.

THEO: "The truth. You are desiring to grow and change, and you are grateful for the gifts that this opportunity—whether it is a friend or a job—has given you, but you are now in a different place."

MARCUS: Sometimes, it ends very naturally and organically.

THEO: "In the past, what has happened is that the employee usually quits doing what they are doing. They become negative, and they create a situation where the employer lets them go. But the true intention is that the employee wanted to be let go and did not have the ability, or the wherewithal, to tell the truth."

MARCUS: Or the courage.

THEO: "Courage, yes. It is true. And in not having that courage, their actions speak louder than their words."

MARCUS: So, talk to us about gaining the courage to be authentic.

THEO: "Begin in one circumstance. Try it out. You will never know unless you try to do it in the elegant manner. To speak your truth; for the truth of your being is the gift you give the world. And most only speak their truth when they can do it in anger. Try it before it gets that severe that you are so uncomfortable."

MARCUS: What do you say to people who just do not seem to be

able to conjure up the courage to do the things that they know they need to do? How do we become courageous?

THEO: "When things become intolerable is when change happens. You have to be uncomfortable enough to change."

MARCUS: So, speaking of change and courage, do we stay in an unhappy marriage for the kids?

THEO: "No. What you are giving them is the dissension, the lack of love and comfortability in the environment. And know these children are not infant souls. They are just smaller bodies, and they chose to be in this environment to learn from it and together with those involved. You are not protecting them by staying together. You are protecting yourself. If the parents are healed, the children will be fine, for what you are modeling for them is an old paradigm, an old way of being, in relationship that they will carry forward in their lives. This is the time for grand change for human experience upon this planet. Be the way-shower of a new way, relinquishing those patterns. For as you do the integrative process, you are changing the lineage of generational patterns that have been passed along for centuries, not just expressing now. You are changing cultural patternings as well that no longer serve the human experience."

MARCUS: Speak more to shifting these cultural patternings.

THEO: "Changing out of the patriarchal position in human experience upon this planet and not just to the matriarchal, because that has been experienced as well. It is the balance of the masculine and feminine energy in each and every one of you and in your relationships, and to experience the joy in that, for it allows for the opportunity of each truth to be known, each individual truth, and the acceptance and self-love to shine forth."

CHAPTER SEVEN

HEALING FROM BETRAYAL

Betrayal is a perception of being harmed in some way with intention that most often is not so. It is an act of unconsciousness."

—THEO

IF WE REALLY ARE co-creators of all our experiences in life, then why would we create encounters that break our hearts and feel as painful as being betrayed? Would you sign up for that class as you were evaluating all the learning possibilities on the menu of life lessons? Most would say no, and yet, we do. Your soul creates events that are in perfect alignment with its intentions for the learning of emotions which are unique to the human experience. In asking a question that begins with why (as we did above), we typically find ourselves in a spiral of victimization, as THEO speaks about in this chapter, in addition to also speaking about how to ask more highly calibrated questions of ourselves and the benefits of doing so. The gifts of compassion, empathy, and wisdom that come from feeling betrayed can be invaluable as you move forward in life, the evidence of which is in abundance in the conversation later in this chapter with THEO and Miriam.

MARCUS: **Define betrayal for us, please.**

THEO: *"Betrayal is an event that one has a feeling of not being heard, not being loved ultimately. The truth has not been given. It is all about truth and honorability and the honoring of another."*

MARCUS: **What is the most common form of betrayal that you observe?**

THEO: *"Most often, it is betrayal that is felt when one has trusted another, and the other has acted upon or spoken untruths."*

MARCUS: **What is our role as co-creators of our lives in creating the betrayal?**

THEO: *"So there is the dance, as we have spoken, of not wanting to hurt someone else's feelings, and so the individual acts from that perspective and withholds their truth, whatever it might be."*

111

MARCUS: **Do we always create that experience for our highest growth?**

THEO: *"You do, although it can be difficult to perceive at the time, but betrayal is a perception when one takes the action of another personally. So, the perception is that they have done something to you."*

MARCUS: **Right, which typically leads to the question "Why is this happening to me?"**

THEO: *"It would—that you are a victim of circumstance."*

MARCUS: **And we are not.**

THEO: *"Correct, but ultimately, one who betrays another is actually betraying themselves."*

MARCUS: **Speak more to that.**

THEO: *"So, they are not doing it to you. They are not doing the betrayal act to you. They are betraying themselves by acting out in a manner that is untruthful, so they are not doing anything to you. The common incorrect perception is that life is happening to you. That you are a victim of circumstance. The truth is that someone is acting out in their own energetic field, their own path, and ultimately, the betrayal is to the self, undermining the trust from others. Yes?"*

MARCUS: **Right. And we know that some questions are more highly calibrated than others. What do you see as the most self-sabotaging questions that we ask ourselves?**

THEO: *"Why questions. You can ask a why question, but the question should be 'Why is this happening for me, not to me?' Anytime one asks 'Why is this happening?' it is pertaining to 'Why am I feeling uncomfortable? I do not want to feel these feelings that are uncomfortable.' But when you look for the answer for the learning, for the experience of the why, ultimately, it is discovery, isn't it?"*

MARCUS: **And the why questions tend to be attached to the feeling that a force outside of ourselves is doing something to us.**

THEO: *"And that is a perception—one that keeps people stuck in their victimization, yes?"*

MARCUS: **Right, so let's talk about asking better questions; who, how, when and where?**

THEO: *"Who have I not met yet? Who do I not know yet? Where do I need to go? Whom do I need to speak to? All of those . . . who, how, where, when questions . . . are questions of discovery, questions of expansion, questions of openness to discover. Yes?"*

MARCUS: **Yes, so, when we are feeling betrayed, what is the first question we should be asking ourselves?**

THEO: *"Why is this happening for me? What is the gift? What is the blessing to be received?"*

MARCUS: **What is the best way to find the gift and the lesson within this?**

THEO: *"To ask the self these questions: 'What are the feelings? Where are they coming from? Who inside of me is uncomfortable? What expectation has gone unmet?'"*

MARCUS: **How do we apply the soul integration principles to healing from betrayal?**

THEO: *"Yes because betrayal is a feeling, and it is a perception of a perceived wrong. 'Is that true?' That is another question to ask the self. 'Is it true?' Have you been betrayed, or is it just a perception of that? And who is perceiving that inside of you?"*

MARCUS: **It may not be true at all.**

THEO: *"Correct. It may be a vibrational frequency that you have experienced before where there has been an experience, and the perception was that something or someone was doing something to you—a repetitive patterning, as it were—but it is coming from an energy emitted by you that you deserve that experience, that you deserve that treatment, if you would, that you are not worthy, yes?"*

MARCUS: **Yes. We tend to turn the questioning to "What is wrong with me?" How do we stay out of that mindset?**

THEO: *"Go a step further. Who inside is uncomfortable? What expectation has gone unmet? When did it first start? When did I first*

*experience this feeling? For it has been experienced before, particu-
larly if you are noticing a pattern reoccurring continuously in life."*

MARCUS: This invites us to look at the beliefs that we hold that may
be manifesting a repetitive pattern of betrayal.

THEO: *"It is all about limiting beliefs. You feel limited in some way, and
it is proving you right."*

MARCUS: I have heard you say that throughout lifetimes, we have
all been both the victim and the perpetrator in this dance of
betrayal.

THEO: *"That is the human experience. Each of you has done actions in
this lifetime, or in previous incarnations, that others may have felt
betrayed by, just as others may act out in a way that is uncomfortable to you. And the perception is that you have been betrayed.
Trust is what is betrayed. Trust should not be freely given but often is,
and when one feels betrayed, you realize trust is something earned,
not freely given."*

MARCUS: How do we trust again after being betrayed?

THEO: *"By communicating with the part of self that holds the distrust."*

MARCUS: That holds that belief.

THEO: *"Yes. It is all about limiting beliefs. Where do they come from?
When did they first start? What is the occurrence? Rewrite that
script so that you can love the self enough where that does not
occur, and in your dialogue and communication with each other, you
let your expectations be known. 'These are the things that matter.
These are my core values. This is what is important to me.' And at
the top of everyone's list is trust."*

MARCUS: How can we heal from betrayal in the shortest period?

THEO: *"By asking the right questions. By seeing who is feeling betrayed.
What part of self is feeling the feelings—the emotionality of it and
the repetition of it—to get to the core circumstance? The revelation
allows you to move through that and change, and letting the self
know that you, the higher self, the adult self, even the future self,
loves this part of you and will not abandon it."*

THEO mentions the benefit of accessing the future self which they define as "The higher self, that which you can see into the future of who you wish to be, who you can be, knowing the possibility of that master that you are." We would add that this is that part of our self that does not worry, has no resistance or fear, and knows without doubt that it all worked out, and that the grief and feelings of betrayal are behind us.

In this next conversation with Miriam, we see her seeking freedom from the trauma of divorce and the shift that takes place about the meaning of love. Conditioned to believe that if I "give, give, give," as she shares with us, that everything would then work out, that that was the right way to love. How much of ourselves do we give up when this is our way of perceiving? With this new awareness that love is equally giving and receiving, she opens herself up now to manifesting a vastly different and much more fulfilling romantic relationship, seeing her divorce not as a failure but as a powerful tool of transformation necessary for accelerated spiritual growth and self-love.

THEO LIVE WITH MIRIAM

MIRIAM: There is something that I am believing that is not allowing myself to be free from the whole trauma from my divorce. What is it that I need to come to accept, to understand, to move forward?

THEO: *"So, as we have stated earlier, the issue of abandonment is extreme. The little girl inside of you was afraid she would be abandoned, looking for that love from the mother, from the parents that was not being achieved. And then you married a person that you assumed loved you because he was very much like your mother. Yes? And you did everything you could. You bent over backwards. You did all the emotional work for him. You created the relationship fully, 100%, for he could not. And so, when the divorce came, the ultimate happened, the abandonment—the thing you were most afraid of, this little one was most afraid of. And you are here, and she did not die. But that is the depth of this. It is not an instantaneous thing, like someone could say to you, 'Well, it has been a year or two years or 20 years,' whatever it has been. It does not matter because it is what it is, and you are moving through it now in this self-realization. It is grief as well, grieving what could have been, what the fantasy you had of it, which was tremendous. He did not do that; you did. But the beauty of this is that you can have that life with someone who can participate because you are giving that to that little girl. You are loving her now. You did not know what you did not know at that time. It was exhausting doing all that work, wasn't it?"*

MIRIAM: I did not know.

THEO: "Yes, you do now."

MIRIAM: I thought that was love.

THEO: "Of course, you did."

MIRIAM: I just gave, gave, gave. I thought that was the right way to love.

THEO: "The intention behind it was to get love as well, wasn't it?"

MIRIAM: Yes.

THEO: "'If I did all of this, I would get something back for it,' and there was nothing to get back for it. You cannot give to someone and expect them to give what they don't have."

MIRIAM: What is loyalty? Is that an expectation?

THEO: "Yes, most often it is. It depends on what your intentions are. But betrayal is difficult as well."

MIRIAM: It hurts. It hurts.

THEO: "It does, but understand this: when somebody betrays you, they will do it to someone else as well because that is who they are. And everyone has been a betrayer and has been betrayed in different lifetimes. It is part of the human experience of learning. But it stems for you in the expectation. For every action, there is a reaction, equally, energetically. So, for every action there is an intention behind it, and it may be an unconscious intention, or subconscious, because most often it is not a realization that 'If I am going to do this for you, I am going to get this back.' That is under the surface. So, the woundedness in you attracted what you thought was love, what you experienced as love. You did not know anything any differently. Now you do."

MIRIAM: Out of this, I feel like I deceived myself in always expecting or just seeing the good, and it puts me now in a place where I feel self-doubt, which I did not feel before.

THEO: "So, we spoke earlier here, did we not, of the same thing? But it is not to judge the self harshly that you perceive in others what they could be, seeing their divinity. It truly is a gift to be able to see that in others. But what is necessary is to see who they are in their human experience as well, and not to want more for them than they want for themselves or can do for themselves, for they may not have had enough human life experiences to understand what that could be yet. So, it is not that they do not want it; they do not even know it is possible. They are incapable of that knowledge. So, you, as a mature soul, chose a young soul to be married to. It sounds simple, doesn't it? But he was not capable of that to the degree that you were, nor was your mother. Most often, you would say, 'Why after all this could they not know?' They just couldn't because they had no experience of it, no understanding of it."

MIRIAM: Out of this, what do I need to see or believe to be able to perceive something positive from my divorce? Until recently, I saw it as a failure, that there was no good in it.

THEO: "There is no failure here, just feedback."

MIRIAM: Just feedback.

THEO: "'I don't want to do that again,' yes? You did not fail at anything. As a matter of fact, you did more than was required. Ultimately you overdid it. But how you get out of where you are now, and feeling *the feelings that you are feeling, is to just feel them. It is grief, and it will not overwhelm you. But, in the judgment of the self, you are feeling that you betrayed yourself. You did not. What has the gift been?"*

MIRIAM: Oh, so many. Really, now that I look back on a lot of things, I used to think that I was codependent and all of that. I understand now how strong and independent I am. I was a single mom for 25 years.

THEO: *"Ahh, there it is! But that is how the mind deceives one—you put so much love into it that you assumed it was coming from him. You created that relationship fully."*

MIRIAM: Not in the next one. I will not carry somebody like that again.

THEO: *"No."*

MIRIAM: I am learning to love myself more.

THEO: *"Loving yourself, but also magnetizing unto yourself, now one of that likeness of the love that you hold for yourself."*

MIRIAM: Yes. Am I healthy in that way right now?

THEO: *"Yes."*

MIRIAM: Okay, good.

THEO: *"You are getting more so every day. Yes?"*

MIRIAM: Yes.

THEO: *"And you are more aware of attracting someone that is similar to your energy now."*

MIRIAM: I would love that.

THEO: *"Yes. One that is not of the old pattern."*

MIRIAM: Yes, for sure.

THEO: *"And you know what that looks like, but talk to that little girl inside you and let her know that you love her with true unconditional love that she didn't know before. This is the last vestige of that grief."*

MIRIAM: Good, I am ready to play!

THEO: *"It is time, isn't it?"*

MIRIAM: It is time! I am so ready for it!

MIRIAM SHARES HER STORY

When I look back on my life and I see the impact that this session had, it is nothing short of miraculous! Wow! This session was perhaps the most impactful ever in my life. It was a shattering eye-opener to remove the veil of my disconnect from within myself.

It has been transformational—to say the least—to be able to understand the lessons and to be able to appreciate the gifts that life experiences bring for the purpose of our inner growth. What a great opportunity for spiritual growth and self-awareness, and ultimately for healing. Impeccable!

I am beyond content on how useful, how educational, and how much understanding I have gained from learning the process of soul integration from THEO.

What a gift it is to stop being the victim and to stop the self-condemnation, to open the doors of my heart to compassion, grace, and mercy.

I am deeply honored for having had the opportunity to participate in the Art of Relationship retreat in such a supportive environment during one of the hardest times in my life—a time of loss and grieving. I am deeply grateful to have experienced this transformation in my life.

MARCUS: How do we begin the process of forgiveness after being betrayed?

THEO: *"Most often, we hear you say that you forgive . . . words, just words, but actions speak louder than words. Feel the feeling of the truth of that. When you go to forgive someone, are you? Or is it just lip service to make the situation more comfortable? You can know by the feeling if it is true forgiveness and the forgiving of the self* first. Oftentimes, there is incrimination of the self for creating the circumstance that brought the betrayal, but how you know there is truth in that forgiveness to the self or to another is how it feels on the inner. Is it true? And if it is not, why not? What we mean by that is: which aspect of the self is still holding on to that energy and why are they holding on to it in such a way that is a disservice to them?"

MARCUS: **So, it is all an inside-out job.**

THEO: "It is."

MARCUS: **What do you mean when you say "inside-out job?"**

THEO: "We are speaking about loving the self on the inner. You have the expectation of finding love externally to fill up the hole inside of you that is feeling undeserving, and so, beings look outside for another to fill that cup on the inner. And it is an impossibility, for they cannot meet your expectations. It is an impossibility. You must meet them for the self by loving the self, filling that cup up inside you by recognizing where the limiting beliefs are and loving the self through it, loving those little aspects of self that feel left behind or frozen in moments of events that diminished you, bringing them forward into the present, into the now, and acknowledging their strengths and offering encouragement and gratitude for assisting you to be the person you are today. So, it is validating them, not separating from them any longer."

MARCUS: **How do we know when we have finally forgiven someone?**

THEO: "It is peace. There is no resistance; there is relief. And you can feel the energy between you that has held that resentment dissolve."

MARCUS: **Ultimately, we are forgiving them for ourselves, aren't we?**

THEO: "You are, yes. And what you are forgiving them for is giving you an opportunity of growth. What we are encouraging you to do is change your perception. Change your mind. The events are not going to change, but your perception of the event can be changed by what you find the gift in it to be. The blessing you received from that event shifts the energy. Instead of looking for the bad, you look for the good."

MARCUS: As the conscious creator of our lives, we are then invited to forgive ourselves for manifesting it in the first place.

THEO: *"It is a vicious circle, isn't it?"*

MARCUS: It is, isn't it? What more can you say about that?

THEO: *"But that is all part of the recrimination of how the fragmentation occurs—the belittling of the self, creating beliefs that you are not worthy or loveable or acceptable, or whatever the not-enoughnesses are—so it perpetuates that story, doesn't it?"*

MARCUS: It does.

THEO: *"Breaking the theme, breaking that mindset, if you would, and laying new neural pathways in your brain from the negative to the positive. When you look for the gifts and the blessings in each situation and circumstance for the opportunity of growth, then you are laying new ways of thinking about it. The brain can only feed certain thoughts in the brain to keep them coherent, and so when you are feeding it the positive, looking for the blessings and the gifts in those opportunities, you are letting go of the victimization, and when the brain releases it, then the new default in the brain is the new neural pathway of blessings."*

MARCUS: Please speak more about creating new neural pathways.

THEO: *"It is how you think. It is the words that you use and the thoughts that you have. If you are continually feeding the belief that you are not loveable, that you are not acceptable, that you are not pretty or handsome, you are not smart, whatever the self-speak is, that is what is feeding the neural pathways of the brain. And it continues to be the default in a reaction to any situation or circumstance. But if you are now validating the self, loving the self, looking for the blessings and gifts . . . 'I am the person who is a divine master being engaging in life with love' . . . that is creating a new neural pathway. Then if that is continuously fed, it locks into the brain in a way that then is continuously fed and the belief and the perception and the words that 'I am not enough' releases from the brain, and the new default system is validation. It is not from an egocentric or narcissistic point of view or self-centeredness but soul-centeredness, and it is expressed in life vibrationally and energetically."*

MARCUS: **Define soul-centeredness for us, THEO.**

THEO: *"It is the calm. As we have spoke that it is like the eye of the hurricane. It is like the calm in the middle of that storm. Whatever conditions or challenges you have, you can be in the centered heart space of self-love and connection."*

MARCUS: **Perhaps the greatest betrayal of all would be to be sexually assaulted. How do we forgive, heal, and move on?**

THEO: *"That is betrayal of the ultimate trust, your creative force, because sexuality is your creative force. Sexuality creates humans, creates babies, doesn't it? And when one invalidates you in such a sacred way, it scars the soul."*

MARCUS: **How do we heal that scar on the soul?**

THEO: *"It is the integrative process. It is loving that part of self. Many have recriminations about blaming the self for those circumstances. But the bad behavior of another does not speak that you are lesser than, particularly when it is one that holds power over another, and that is an act of violence."*

MARCUS: **That was my next question—of being abused by a priest, for instance.**

THEO: *"Not only is that a negative in the sense of taking power over another, which is inappropriate, but it is also one's spirituality and God-connectedness, so it is more powerful, or the trust of a parent or a loved one. So, it undermines trust, doesn't it? The most sacred trust."*

MARCUS: **Right. So, how do we heal from that?**

THEO: *"You are the best one, the higher self of you, the adult self, to heal that little one inside, letting it know it is loved and will not be abandoned or harmed again. You will take care of it. Know it is frozen in that moment of experience. So, what you are doing is unthawing them to come forward into your current time in life, a time now of love and protection, and letting them know that they did nothing wrong, for most recriminate and say, 'It is my fault.'"*

MARCUS: **You mentioned that it scars the soul. What does that mean?**

THEO: *"It separates."*

MARCUS: **So that is the fragmentation.**

THEO: *"It's fragments."*

MARCUS: **So, the scarring of the soul is when an aspect of the soul fragments during a traumatic experience. Talk about the higher self coming in at that point.**

THEO: *"The higher self comes in, the adult self, to maintain life and take over. When this aspect or this fragment occurs at a certain age, it freezes that part of self from that moment that they have the inability to act."*

MARCUS: **And then we make a connection with that aspect of self that went through the experience. And that is where the healing occurs?**

THEO: *"Yes. What is felt is relief and love, and there may be tears, an emotionality. Let that flow. It is part of the release and relief."*

MARCUS: **Is healing from betrayal any different than healing from any other kinds of grief?**

THEO: *"Some may feel betrayed if someone leaves them in death because the ultimate fear is abandonment. And what happens to herd animals if they are ostracized, set aside without community, without love? They die. They are not supported. It has been proven in science with humans and infants that if they are not nurtured and touched and connected to, they do not live long."*

MARCUS: **Does time really heal?**

THEO: *"Those are good words. Yes, but what time does is give you different perceptions."*

MARCUS: **Is it possible to collapse time in the healing process?**

THEO: *"There is when you take responsibility for it."*

MARCUS: **Speak more to that.**

THEO: *"Rather than being stuck in the story of your victimization, you can ask those calibrated questions—of who, what, where, when, how—to give you the clarity and the ability to know that then you, the higher self of you, the adult self, can soothe, comfort, and love those aspects of self that hold the beliefs of not being worthy."*

MARCUS: **You have mentioned many times the need to occasionally access the future self. What does that mean?**

THEO: *"When there is a fragmented aspect of the soul that is closer in age to the adult, the soul can be enmeshed energetically as one, creating no distance for observation. So, calling on the future self that has been through that moment of discomfort and is on the other side of it with greater wisdom can come forth and take over."*

MARCUS: **It is hard for us with our linear perception of time to get our head around the concept of the future self. Speak more to how we can access and use the energy of the future self to assist us in our present moment.**

THEO: *"You first have to believe it. You all have the imaginations where you can see yourself in the future. If you are going to move to a new house, you see yourself making the move. You perceive that, don't you? You are going to a new job; you can perceive yourself going to that building, going into a new job before you get there. Can you not? So that is the perception we are talking about. You can call forth the perception of going through this moment into the next, one minute ahead, two minutes ahead even, and you have already discovered and moved through that uncomfortable moment. That is the future self that can give you the information you are asking for."*

MARCUS: **I have heard you describe it as remembering the future.**

THEO: *"Yes."*

MARCUS: **I think I have even heard you quote "Alice in Wonderland."**

THEO: *"We have. It is a poor memory that only goes backwards."*

MARCUS: **What have I not asked you on the topic of healing from betrayal?**

THEO: "The words that are given are simple words. It is in the action, in the commitment in the decision to heal . . . that is where the energy lies . . . and you have the ability to do that."

CHAPTER EIGHT

HAVEN'T WE MET SOMEWHERE BEFORE?

*"Beings incarnate together purposefully
to support each other's growth."*

—THEO

HAVE YOU EVER HAD an experience of meeting someone for the first time and feeling such a vibrational resonance, a visceral feeling so comfortable, that you thought "Wow, it is remarkable that we finally met up again in this lifetime"? That you felt such an immediate energetic connection that you must have known each other in a previous incarnation? Many have, and when you do, it opens the heart and mind to knowing that you have lived before in the human experience and will again if you choose to. But, as we ask THEO in this chapter, if we have a soul contract with someone, how in the world do we find each other amongst almost eight billion other souls on this planet? We only have our personal experience, as we shared in chapter 1, to answer this question; it appears we just do. How the other souls in the play gather somehow in their perfect time also remains a mystery for now.

Another interesting phenomenon occurs prior to souls incarnating. We have heard numerous stories of mothers [and grandmothers!] who have been contacted prior to the birth with important messages from the unborn. While I was thinking about this topic, I was reminded of the time in May 1990, before the birth of my oldest grandson, when he came to me with a specific request about what he wanted his name to be. My daughter Stephanie and her husband Dennis were expecting their first child and had decided they did not want to know the gender of their baby, so even though I intuitively knew they were having a boy, I did not inform them of what I knew. This knowing became even more difficult to keep to myself when this unborn soul came to me while I was driving to the grocery store one morning three weeks before he was born to confirm for me that he was a boy and that he wanted his name to be Andrew. I assured him I would share his request with his parents.

When I returned home, I called Stephanie and just blurted out,

"Your baby is a boy, and he wants his name to be Andrew." There was a long pause before she acknowledged that she knew she was having a boy and that Dennis had just stopped by her office to tell her that he thought that they should name the baby Andrew.

Three weeks later, Andrew was born, and two weeks after that, I met him for the first time in human form. I was sitting on the sofa holding him on my lap, he lying flat on his back with his head on my knees and his cute little feet on my belly. He looked so clear-eyed and alert, and I said to him, "You did it. You got your name to be Andrew." He looked me straight in the eyes and laughed out loud. I share this with you as an example of how souls choose their families and how we make soul contracts with each other prior to incarnating. The other thing I know for sure is that I recognized Andrew the moment I looked in his eyes.

MARCUS: Would you please define soul contract, or agreement?

THEO: "Groups incarnate together to support each other's growth. So, the first contract is that you gather and incarnate at the same time. There are specific soul contracts for a particular learning experience, and so oftentimes, that is why one has chosen a family in which they are the persons they have contracts with expressed in that dynamic. There are other contracts. There are contracts of marriage. There are contracts of relationships of friendships and of work mates. So, there is an agreement to come together to learn particular experiences together and to learn from and with one another."

MARCUS: How do souls perceive the human experience prior to incarnation—and what is the communication among souls?

THEO: "So there is a desire in the individual soul for a particular learning to be achieved and experienced, a greater understanding of human feelings. So, in that dialogue it may be 'I will go if you go.' It is as simple as that. We will achieve this together as teams, to support people, each other, to learn particular emotions."

MARCUS: It feels almost magical, THEO, that we somehow find each other amongst almost eight billion people residing on our planet today.

THEO: "Yes. Understand this: you know if you have a reaction to anybody, whether it is positive or negative, when you meet them, you can ascertain that you have known each other before. Recognize out of the tens of thousands of people that you cross paths within a lifetime, how many are you truly attracted to? Very few, comparatively speaking. Yes?"

MARCUS: Right. So, is there a hierarchy of some kind directing, or does each individual soul make its own choice to incarnate?

THEO: "There is not a demand made upon you at all. It is all choice. One is not greater than another. It is by agreement. Yes?"

MARCUS: Right, so can these contracts or agreements be changed?

THEO: "They can be completed. The dynamic of how you do them can change. Yes."

MARCUS: How does our free will influence these changes or when to complete them?

THEO: "You complete them . . . that changes everything . . . and in a completed contract, the souls may choose to continue in the relationship or not. That is where the change or a change in agreement can occur."

MARCUS: THEO, how do you define soul family?

THEO: "Soul family is beings that are on the same vibrational frequency. Souls are eternal, and that you are aligned on a vibrational match, that is a continuum."

MARCUS: Is this just in the human experience that we come together, or do we also collaborate in other dimensions, other planets, or other experiences?

THEO: "You work in other dimensions and other planets and other situations and circumstances. The Earth is only one choice. There are billions of choices."

MARCUS: How do you define "sacred friends," the term the Dalai Lama uses to describe the Chinese Government?

THEO: *"They are your greatest teachers, for they are giving you the opportunity of that growth."*

MARCUS: Can they be soul family?

THEO: *"They can."*

MARCUS: They seem to be the ones that are the most challenging in this lifetime, but as you say, they are our greatest teachers.

THEO: *"They are. How do you learn best? It is through challenge, isn't it? You take ease for granted, but when you are challenged, your senses are heightened, looking for resolution, looking for solutions, growth, understanding. You are uncomfortable, and so you are looking for a change. That is where the learning comes."*

MARCUS: THEO, is there anything that is random?

THEO: *"It appears that there is, but know there is a linkage energetically in the quantum field for all things."*

MARCUS: Speak more to that.

THEO: *"It is hard for you to think about, but understand when you are living a life, there is energy that is flowing in and through and around you at all times. That is the manifestational energy that is called the quantum field. And so, there is a particular alignment to all of the outcomes that happen in life—the people you meet, the opportunities for growth.*

MARCUS: What would you say to those that are feeling alone on their spiritual journey?

THEO: *"That is a choice, isn't it?"*

MARCUS: What if they do not feel it is a choice? That they do not desire to be alone?

THEO: *"Then make an intention for it, a decision for it. 'I am the man or woman who draws unto me those of like-mindedness in relationships. I am open and receptive to receive those relationships.'"*

MARCUS: Speak more to this please.

THEO: *"By intention of drawing forth unto the self those of like minds, and it may be a weeding of the garden, as we have spoken about of old relationships, freeing the energy for the new to come forward."*

MARCUS: How do we consciously attract our spiritual community, our soul family?

THEO: *"Intend it, as we stated. Making it welcome. Opening the heart for that to occur. I am the person who draws unto me now like-minded relationships. And first, do the integrational process to see where the resistance lies for that to occur in your life."*

MARCUS: It is really a process of getting to know ourselves, isn't it?

THEO: *"It is."*

MARCUS: What if we are shy or uncomfortable socially?

THEO: *"As many are. So, talk to who inside of you is shy or uncomfortable, and then support them. The higher self can support these little aspects of self that feel fearful. The what-if they do not like me. Well, what if they do not? There is someone who does and will be a part of your group, your connection. If you are not a vibrational match for those that you are aligning with, there are those who will be. Trust that."*

MARCUS: What do you say to people who just feel lonely?

THEO: *"Who feels lonely? It is not the whole self that feels lonely. There is an aspect of self that there is an expectation. Who inside is resistant to that filling up the self, the loving of self? For one can be with a large group of people and still be lonely. It does not have anything to do with being around others. It is all an inner process."*

MARCUS: THEO, how would you define the dark night of the soul?

THEO: *"It is a challenge. It feels dark to people who are highly challenged. Engaging and calling forth and understanding on a soul level the challenge and grasping the opportunity of the growth therein."*

MARCUS: What if the awareness of the growth within is not present in that moment?

THEO: *"So you will be in it until it becomes intolerable, and then you begin asking the questions."*

MARCUS: You've mentioned that there are different soul ages. What determines one's soul age, and what are the characteristics of young souls and old souls?

THEO: "The different ages of the soul have to do with incarnations in human experience. We are not talking about the total soul. We are talking about the human experience of the soul. So, there may be souls that have not previously chosen the earthly plane as a place to engage with, and then they do. They could be defined as a young soul or a new soul. That is only new to the human experience. It does not mean the soul is not eternal. It is just the choice of the human experience on the earthly plane has not been as many as an old soul, let us say. So, a young soul is new to the human experience. An adolescent soul has had a few more lifetimes than the young soul, just as there is maturation of the human body from infancy to old age. So, there is a maturation, a maturing that happens through experience, just like life matures. However, in a young soul, their awareness of the human experience does not change in one lifetime. It changes in several. So, the young souls often come; they have no idea or the ability to have compassion or interaction or understanding of the human experience. And so they are acting out from a self-centered, egotistical, and self-absorbed way. Adolescent souls do the same because they have had enough life experience but still use manipulation and different things in their human life to begin to learn to have compassion. So how they interact is from that arrogance of adolescence. Then there is a mature soul who has had several human lifetimes and has learned compassion through the challenges they have met in the human body, in the human life existence. And then the older soul who is one who has had many, even many hundreds of human experiences, has learned greater emotions, has learned how to navigate emotions, and has a greater aptitude for compassion, just through experience."

MARCUS: What is the best way to use this knowledge to understand and interact with people better?

THEO: "What helps to understand is if you are expecting a particular person to act differently, there is an expectation because they are a mature human to act in a certain way. But their soul age is such that they have not the tools or the capability to act as a mature and older soul of what you see. They are still in their infancy or adolescence. So, for an example, the older soul is at the university or graduate level, and a younger soul is at the kindergarten level. You would not expect a five-year-old or a kindergartener who has just started the educational system to know and understand the precepts and concepts that a university student does. They just have not had enough education yet. Are they incapable of it? No, they just have not been shown the way."

MARCUS: Sounds like you are describing the benefit of lowering expectations.

THEO: "For an example, if an older soul has a parent that is an infant, a younger soul, or even an adolescent soul and expecting them to have the compassion and understanding of a graduate student and they are still in kindergarten in their soul-knowing of the human experience, it can lessen the expectation that they do what one wants them to do in the emotional spectrum."

MARCUS: THEO, do we ever evolve out of the human experience as a soul?

THEO: "The human experience is a choice. You are evolved even if you have never had one. It is just a different experience. It is the learning of emotions. So, there are other places you may choose as a soul, not the earthly plane, but still there is the evolution of the understanding and awareness of whatever the soul chooses to experience and express."

MARCUS: If we become fully soul-integrated, enlightened, in this lifetime, how does that show up if we choose to come back again?

THEO: "As a teacher."

MARCUS: No lost ground?

THEO: "No. You retain all the learnings that you gain."

MARCUS: On the eternal journey of the soul, what does the soul gain by the learning of emotions—the learnings of emotions over all lifetimes?

THEO: *"It is much more expanded in knowledge, has the wisdom of emotions, has the knowledge of the human experience and the navigation of the human body, the earth suit. But also, the Earth is a beautiful planet, and you retain that awareness of its beauty."*

MARCUS: What more is there to share about finding our soul family?

THEO: *"You always will, and there is no doubt when you meet that connection. It is viscerally felt, as well as intellectually known."*

MARCUS: What more is there on the topic of soul ages and contracts that I have not asked you?

THEO: *"We would prefer for you to know not to be stuck in your head about it. Most people, instead of living it, stay in the intellectual aspect, and what is most important is that you work from the heart, the emotional seat of the soul, to the head.*

MARCUS: Tell us more about that.

THEO: *"The head, the intellect, is a problem-solver, and it likes to control any situation. And for humans, for souls in human bodies, control is extremely important for most, for it means survival. So, when one goes to the heart for the response first in how to respond to life, rather than the head, there is a different level of compassion that occurs in the life experience. It is the process of integration—feeling the feeling of that peace, the soul centered within, and it is a process of personal growth and change—they are all connected energetically."*

Gail's experience with THEO illuminates for us the purposefulness of every relationship—that there are no mistakes, even when it appears otherwise. That as we look back on our relationships, we can see that we magnetized to us precisely the vibrational match we were ourselves at that time, and that there is no reason to beat ourselves up or have any regrets when we recognize the great learning and growth in each experience. That they were all contributing to our soul growth.

THEO LIVE WITH GAIL

GAIL: I was speaking with my coaching client this morning, and she has left her husband. She says he was the perfect man to have her children with, and she was glad she did that. But they are no longer a match. I believe that they were never a match because she always said that she saw potential in him. And I am divorced and chose a good man to have children with but not as a mate. Can you speak to that kind of relationship and why that happened?

THEO: "It was a good relationship at the time. It was a match for her and for you, or it would not have happened. But you both grew in different directions. If you recognize that human life used to have a short span and individuals would marry and then they died in a few years. What has occurred now is that the lifespan has tripled and more still, more than that even. So, you have many lifetimes in one incarnation."

GAIL: So, it is not a failure or not the way that it is meant to be, to be in multiple relationships throughout our life.

THEO: "It depends on the person, for there are some who have one relationship for an entire lifetime of many, many years."

GAIL: And some are happy, and some are not.

THEO: "Yes. But who dictates that? But in this circumstance to say a perfect person to have children with but not to live with. You did live together, did you not? And we are speaking of the other person. It is the same. And there were many things that occurred that made you who you are today in that interaction of relationship and family. It was just complete."

GAIL: What about souls choosing their parents? After I split up with my husband, I found out that I was pregnant with a fourth child.

The pregnancy caused my husband to come back and stay for another three years. The pregnancy terminated because I got chicken pox at age 32, and the pregnancy did not last. But he stayed around for three years. Was there a soul that did this orchestration to bring us back together for a while?

THEO: *"That would be a nice excuse, wouldn't it? No. But the situation and circumstance did; the soul did not. For the soul did not come to fruition, did it? The infant was not born, but the experience of that brought you back together because the relationship had not truly completed yet. We find it interesting the words, split up, split up. There was a choosing to go on different paths. You are still connected."*

GAIL: We are still very connected . . . three children.

THEO: *"Yes. And you have seen the goodness in that."*

GAIL: Yes, I have seen the goodness in him.

THEO: *"Excellent because you are able to see the goodness in yourself. One cannot see that in another if they cannot see it in themselves, because the beliefs about the self color the lenses in which you see life and others through."*

GAIL: When I was married to him, I felt a lot of anger and almost a hatred towards him, probably because I felt it in myself at the time. Now that I have grown, I can even love him.

THEO: *"Yes."*

GAIL: Okay. Thank you.

GAIL SHARES HER EXPERIENCE

THEO's answer helped me realize that I did not make a mistake by marrying my husband. For most of my life, I had felt like I had chosen the wrong person, and that is why my marriage had failed. I could not see it as a regret because we created three wonderful children together, but I wondered about my choice. THEO explained that my choice was a match at the time, and that it was meant to be. Or we would not have connected. And that in the end, it was not a failure but a completion. I was very relieved and felt a weight lift and now am ready to go forward and live the next parts of my life.

THEO also explained that the baby I miscarried did not have a soul because the pregnancy did not come to fruition. I had always wondered if there was a little soul out there still waiting for me, and I can now be relieved to know that souls enter at birth.

My thoughts about my life before the THEO teachings and conversations were I got it wrong. I have failed. I missed the mark.

These thoughts have been transformed by studying with The THEO Group. I now realized that I could not have possibly gotten my life wrong. That it all unfolded perfectly imperfectly. That I did not miss any opportunities that were meant for me. That the people and events in my life were all to teach and inform me. That my life is always evolving and expanding and aligning for my highest good.

CHAPTER NINE

How in the World Did I End Up in This Family?

"Birth family is the incarnated source of agreement one unto the other for a particular purpose."

—*THEO*

BY NOW YOU HAVE probably concluded that every relationship is purposeful in its own unique way and that there is an opportunity for growth and learning within every interaction. This may be most true with the birth family you chose to incarnate with. Imagine your family all getting together before this lifetime and making agreements for each soul's learning. And that the lessons will not always be fun to experience.

You may not resonate, or even have a relationship, with certain members of your family. You might be close to one parent and have a strained relationship with the other. You may have chosen to incarnate in a family that is highly dysfunctional, without love. Or not. Whatever circumstances you chose, however, the learning is great, even if you feel like the black sheep of the family—that no one "gets you," which is often the case if you chose to explore metaphysics or spiritualism and turn away from the religion you were raised in.

This understanding that there are no victims, just volunteers, that family selection is a soul choice, leads us into the awareness that life is happening for us, never to us.

The notion that we pick our families doesn't always go over well when there is discord or disagreement with a family member. I remember telling my then 5-year-old daughter when she was mad at me that she picked me as her father. She immediately told me that she would never have picked me as her dad! So much for trying to get a 5-year-old to take responsibility for her soul choice.

MARCUS: **How do we choose our birth family prior to incarnating?**
THEO: "By choosing, by making a decision for, by agreement with those whom you have incarnated with. Meaning, that there is an agreement of those members of the family that you come into and that

you are going to express your souls' paths together, but it may not be with all. The agreement may be your contract with one or all of them. It is individually soul chosen and group soul choosing. So, there are some circumstances in which the nuclear family or the genetic family are soul family as well, but oftentimes not."

MARCUS: **What do you say to those that wonder "How in the world did I end up in this family?"**

THEO: "Those are the ones we are speaking about that are not soul family—that there is a choosing of a vibrational frequency with one or more members of that family, but not all, for a particular path of the soul's learnings. It is by agreement that you come together."

MARCUS: **What do you say to those that just do not feel a soulful connection at all—to their parents, their siblings, or even to their own children?**

THEO: "Know this: the soul chooses perfectly, and oftentimes, it is the most challenging one that is the reason they are in that family. For where you learn best is when you are challenged, and the soul connection to the one who challenges you is the gift and the reason you are there."

MARCUS: **So, what do you see as the new paradigm within the family dynamic?**

THEO: "In actuality, there is nothing that is new."

MARCUS: **So, there isn't an old way and a new way now to be in family relationships?**

THEO: "No, it has always been a choosing of the soul to be in the environment for its highest good and learning."

MARCUS: **What do you see as the biggest mistake we make within our family relationships?**

THEO: "The expectation that you must like each other. That there is a requisite that you like each other to be in that family. Respecting one another is important, and you do not have to like the personality. But ultimately there is the love of the soul."

MARCUS: **What would you say to those who have been raised by parents who were incapable of loving?**

THEO: *"There was that expectation in many generations in the past. There was a certain perception because you were together that meant you were loved. There are those who do not know how to show love or to experience or to express it, for they have not learned how. There has been a generational patterning of distance. So, that would be thought of as love by the infant for it knows nothing else, and in that environment, there has been no way of learning a new way."*

MARCUS: **So, how do we as parents pattern love for our children when we were not shown that ourselves?**

THEO: *"It is consciousness, isn't it? So, what would you give that child inside of you? For it is you to truly be the parent to your inner child— that part of self formed from the expectation that was never met. What does that child need to hear to be validated and to know they are loved? What would you tell your child, knowing what you know?"*

MARCUS: **It is just developing awareness, isn't it?**

THEO: *"It is, yes. So, if you have not had that patterning, whom do you admire? For there are people that you have watched, that you have admired their interactions with their children, and you can adopt those positive influences."*

MARCUS: **How do we not adopt our parents' limiting beliefs?**

THEO: *"It is difficult. You adopt them to survive within that structure, do you not?"*

MARCUS: **Right, that is why I am asking.**

THEO: *"So, when you have the ability and know that it is not a necessity to stay under that roof, and you have the ability to learn and expand in yourself and understand that you have a mind, you have experiences that have informed you to a new way of thinking."*

MARCUS: **How do we become nonattached to the approval or the good opinions of our parents, or do we ever?**

THEO: "We see that most do not for there is always the striving to be loved by a parent."

MARCUS: And if they had been incapable of showing us love, we still sometimes seem to hang onto that desire, that expectation.

THEO: "You always do. The child is always wanting to, and that is a part of who you are."

MARCUS: How do we find peace around that?

THEO: "By giving that love unto the self and to the fragmented aspect of your soul."

MARCUS: Just replace the love.

THEO: "Yes. But it does not mean that you cannot love that parent as they are."

MARCUS: How do we find peace if we are estranged from our parents or our children?

THEO: "When you get into the state of unconditional love, you will realize that the person is more important than the thing that has estranged you, unless it has been by authority abuse. That is different. That is a different dynamic. But for most who have not had that dynamic—and it is an intellectual choice, or feelings have been hurt, or whatever might be—communication can clear it. But one must ask, 'Is the thing, the expectation, unmet for you more important than the person?'"

MARCUS: What I am hearing in that is forgiveness.

THEO: "It is forgiveness. And realizing that in things and in experiences, communication can heal, but it is. Also, what is your opinion about it? What is your belief about it? What is your perception about the event or circumstance? Can that be changed? You are the only one that knows. But understand this: when you shift your thought pattern, your belief pattern, your understanding to their soul or to the person being more important than any event, thing, or circumstance, then it shifts the blame and the judgment."

MARCUS: Just to keep in mind that love is the main thing.

THEO: "What would love do? And being aware of what their intention was. If you have been so grieved, ask 'Is it true?' For understand this: what is important in any action is the intention behind it. Did they intend to hurt or harm you in any way? Was that their intention to do so? There is a difference when it is intended to harm instead of it being unconscious."

MARCUS: When our soul chooses to be in a family without love, how can we tap into the higher purpose for having chosen that type of family dynamic?

THEO: "Having knowledge. Being informed. Asking the good questions. Not 'why' in a victimized way, but where did this choice come from? What am I to learn in this circumstance, this condition, this family, this opportunity of growth?"

MARCUS: What is the best way to forgive and forget when we feel wronged by a family member?

THEO: "Talk about the proverbial elephant in the room between you, yes? It separates you from love, doesn't it? Communication is your friend, not a foe. Speak. Allow for the ability for vulnerability—'that hurt my feelings.' But the event, the circumstance, the word, whatever it is, was the action leading to the perception of being harmed. So, ask if that was intended? What an interesting concept to communicate rather than to assume. So, if the intention were to hurt you, that is a different energy, isn't it?"

MARCUS: It is, and we can simply choose not to be in that person's life.

THEO: "You can choose that. But what if they said, 'Yes, in that moment, it was my intention, and I am sorry.' That is a different energy as well, yes?"

MARCUS: So, how do we know when it is time to just let go of family members?

THEO: "It depends upon your attitude, doesn't it? There are those that would say, 'I am cutting them off. They are dead to me. I am not going to talk to them.' That is a different way of letting go, isn't it?"

MARCUS: It sounds angry.

THEO: "It is. There are unresolved issues."

MARCUS: **Right. And left unresolved they will stay with us, won't they?**

THEO: "Yes. Ultimately, it harms you more than them, yes?"

MARCUS: **Yes, because we carry the energy with us.**

THEO: "Continuously it is running around in your head all the time and taking up space in your mind."

MARCUS: **We hang onto grudges too.**

THEO: "Many do, yes."

MARCUS: **How can we let go of grudges and old wounds, and reframe history?**

THEO: "Ask, 'How does it serve you? Is it making your life better to do so?' And some get more out of their story in reliving repeatedly than they do in changing it because they receive greater attention, possibly, for it."

MARCUS: **What is ancestral healing?**

THEO: "That is what we talk about. When you integrate, you are letting go of patterning that has been generationally passed along, even culturally, so that is what it is."

MARCUS: **So, soul integration is ancestral healing.**

THEO: "It is."

MARCUS: **Is it possible for us to re-pattern our DNA?**

THEO: "Yes, just like you can lay new neural pathways in your mind."

MARCUS: **What more can you add about our ability to shift our DNA so that we are not victims of our genetic blueprint?**

THEO: "Do your spiritual work. Do your integrative work. Pay attention. Take responsibility for you in your life experience. All of this as you change and transform releases the energy in your physical body that gets stuck and creates disease and illness. If the body's energy is flowing appropriately, without blockage, there is no aging, and there is a shift in what you speak of DNA, for there is no energy there that creates an imbalance in it."

MARCUS: **Speak more to that.**

THEO: *"If you do not release energy and beliefs that hold you back, that are unloving, or that are held in the events of the past, it pools in the body in certain areas of weakness that creates an imbalance that you call illness."*

MARCUS: **You do not see illness in us, do you?**

THEO: *"No, we only see imbalances that can be corrected."*

MARCUS: **And we can do it ourselves?**

THEO: *"Yes. But you have assistance. You have medical professionals. You have alternative and allopathic medical models. The humans have been given this to assist them. One is not greater than the other. The combination of them gives you a full health spectrum and tools to have it."*

MARCUS: **Let's talk about addictions. Please speak about responding to a family member with addictions with love and compassion instead of blame and judgment?**

THEO: *"You do not know what the soul's learning is to be, so judging them for that is inappropriate. You may be in judgment of their actions toward you in their state of addiction. That is different than judging their addiction. That is theirs to deal with, not yours. Yours is only in holding your boundaries to have respectful treatment."*

MARCUS: **If we are addicted, how can we utilize your soul integration principles to heal our own addiction?**

THEO: *"An addiction is an emptiness inside that one is trying to fill up with whatever they are addicted to whether it is food or alcohol or drugs or sex or spending money, and many more. That is just a way of feeling better momentarily. So, notice what you are noticing. What are you filling up on the inner? How can you fill that space with unconditional love of self? It is the integrational process—soothing, comforting those little fragmented aspects that have been wounded and healing those wounds."*

MARCUS: **Are we all a little bit addicted?**

THEO: *"Humans are, yes—in whatever form—some with greater severity than others."*

MARCUS: Is there anything more about how soul integration can assist in healing addictions?

THEO: *"When one is comfortable in their own skin, they are not seeking external stimulus to make them feel better."*

Other than losing a child, there is probably nothing more heartbreaking than having a child suffer from addiction. Or in Kim's case, having two children addicted that are also living with her. And because they are our kids, we would do anything for them, right? As we see in this session, the best thing is not always the easy thing, particularly when it comes to establishing and maintaining necessary, non-negotiable boundaries. These boundaries lead to taking personal responsibility (the ability to respond) and accountability, which are amongst the greatest gifts we can give our kids, addicted or not. It also speaks to the wisdom of not doing—not doing for them that which they need to do for themselves, allowing them to gain the wisdom from having their personal experience of not having it done for them. We know, as parents ourselves, this is sometimes easier said than done.

When we followed up with Kim about a year after the retreat, we were thrilled to hear how her life had changed. The lesson she taught all of us: when we commit to our own spiritual growth and the raising of our personal vibrational frequency, it impacts those around us in unimaginable ways. Her commitment to loving herself resulted in her sons having no choice, as she says, but to do the same!

THEO LIVE WITH KIM

KIM: Two of my adult sons suffer from addiction, and they are still living with me.

THEO: *"Hold boundaries. Require them to show up in a way that you wish them to be in your home, and if they do not, they must go somewhere else. The freedom you are seeking is the boundaries you must hold, and that is difficult to do because you have fear about that."*

KIM: They are my kids; I love them and want them to be okay. And as a mother, I see that they are not okay. So, it is a big fear. You don't want your kids dead under a bridge. When you deal with addiction, you would rather have them dead in their bed as a mom. I think that is a big issue, and yet somehow, I have got to deal with these two kids in my house.

THEO: *"Get help. Get someone to help you understand and see more clearly what is in the best interest of them. For holding fear for them, and sadness and grief, is not serving them. Boundaries. Making them responsible. And that is the chaos you are feeling. You do not know where to go. It is not about your life; it is about theirs, yes?"*

KIM: Yes, if they would just start living their lives. They need to do something.

THEO: *"Allowing them just to be in your home doing what they are doing is not a gift you are giving them or yourself. So, what can you do to change it?"*

KIM: I need to have a meeting with them and talk because that is all I can really come up with.

THEO: *"That is a good beginning. Holding boundaries. The rules of the house. Their participation, work, rent, all the things to live life as an adult. So, that is a meeting you have. They may not like it and may act out as children, but do not let that sway you. The gift you are giving them is structure, just like when you told them to eat their dinner. It was a structure they needed to grow and to thrive. So, this is the next step to the freedom you are seeking and for their well-being. Can they do it? Yes, they can. Both are very smart, and they can do it. They can do it with structure and assistance with programs that will assist them in releasing their addictions, and that should be part of the protocol that they have to be a resident in that home. Yes?"*

KIM: Yes, that makes sense.

THEO: *"And that will give you a sense of order that is so important to* you. Be strong because they are going to try to wiggle out of every-thing. Yes?"

KIM: Yes, they do. They always do.

THEO: "So, you already know that. So, if you are looking at them as a four-year-old stomping their feet, rolling on the ground to get what they want, then you will be stronger, won't you?"

KIM: Yes, I will.

THEO: "You can ignore that and stay firm. So, now you know."

KIM: Okay. Thank you.

KIM SHARES HER EXPERIENCE

Last year, I decided to attend the Art of Relationship work-shop with THEO. I did not have any expectations and went for the experience. I never dreamed I would be sitting across from Sheila and speaking with THEO. It was otherworldly, and I found myself having an experience with truth.

My marriage of 25 years had ended, and I was living with my two adult sons, ages 21 and 18, who were suffering terribly with drug addiction. They were destroying their lives and mine as well. As a mother, I had tried everything to "help" them, and nothing was working. Friends and family had insisted I throw them out. My worst fear was having them die on the street. I was dealing with wrecked cars, legal trouble, drug dealing; the list goes on and on. I know so many families who have lost children to drug overdose in my own town.

As I sat in the mesmerizing presence of THEO, I was receiving practical, helpful advice as well as hope and encour-agement from these loving angelic beings.

I returned home from Arizona after my weekend with THEO and soon discovered I was beginning to have a rela-tionship with myself! I never knew this was something people had, so I began listening to many of the THEO recordings in the AskTHEO library. They were profoundly transformational.

I have spent the last year working on healing and loving myself, and I stopped trying to change my children. As my vibration rose, it was as if my sons had no choice but to improve as well. Less than a year later, they are currently clean and employed! As a result of attending the workshop, I have grown to love myself and look forward to my continued growth.

MARCUS: **Please speak to us about interacting with controlling people.**

THEO: *"It means survival. One desires to survive. They are in an environment that is not safe, so that part of self steps forward and holds boundaries, sometimes in the extreme, to feel safe. So, talk about it, and hold your boundaries of what is inappropriate and appropriate behavior and the power of the word no. No is a sentence, isn't it? 'Yes' is as well."*

MARCUS: **So, it is all about feeling safe?**

THEO: *"Safe, yes. It is all about survival. 'Am I going to die in this situation?' For the soul in the human body desires to live."*

MARCUS: **If we recognize ourselves as being controlling, what would your guidance be?**

THEO: *"Ask, 'Why am I controlling? Who is controlling inside of me? Where does the need to control originate?'"*

MARCUS: **Shifting to parenting, Sheila's friend Virginia Satir taught that if you heal the parents, the kids are going to be fine.**

THEO: *"That is true. That is the process that is at hand now—changing generational patterns that have been passed along for centuries. Generation after generation acting out in the manners of the past. So, as the adults recognize those patterns and heal from the inside out, love the self fully and express that love, the children will not need to carry forward those generational patterns. They will not* misconstrue what is love by the generational patterning that has been exhibited. New patterns can be formed independent of those generations."

MARCUS: How do we keep from collapsing boundaries with our children?

THEO: "It is important to maintain boundaries with them because it teaches them how to have them for themselves, enhancing their own self-respect. Know this: as a parent you are giving structure to a child that allows them to feel safe. It is not something you are doing to them to deprive them of whatever they want. It is to show them a way that they have safety in this structure of respecting the self. So, when presented in the outer world experiences that challenge them, they have something to rely upon, a structure, a form, a foundation of strength in which they can say no and hold boundaries for themselves. Loving the self. Children are looking for safety that someone will take care of them, care for them as they grow, for they do not know everything yet in the human experience, do they? So, a parent does not do for them but allows them to step into that world by letting them know that they have a foundation and structure within that they will not be harmed."

MARCUS: We also have a tendency as parents to step in and do for our children, which essentially deprives them of their own personal learning and growth from that experience.

THEO: "You are taking the gift from them. You think you are giving them the gift by doing for them, but where is the learning for them in their own decision making and having the consequences of that decision? That is the learning. But many parents want to deprive them of the experience for they do not want them to feel the uncomfortable feelings. You are depriving them of feeling that. All beings are here to experience the spectrum of feelings. They are not good or bad. They are what they are, and that is the learning of the soul. And the uncomfortable ones are the greatest gift, for that is where compassion and empathy come from."

MARCUS: **Define tough love.**

THEO: *"Holding boundaries, simply."*

MARCUS: **And it certainly does not change when our children become adults.**

THEO: *"Of course not, because they will still look to you as the parent."*

MARCUS: **Sometimes it is even harder with adult children.**

THEO: *"For some, it is if they have never held boundaries before. It is extremely difficult to start when they are adults."*

MARCUS: **Let's talk more about that.**

THEO: *"So, not to have boundaries with a child and to allow them to do whatever they want to do and then decide to hold the boundary, they don't understand. It is not a gift you give them to collapse boundaries. You do not have to be rigid. You do not have to be making the consequence so large. Pay attention to the offense. Does it equate to the consequence being equal energetically? For many have an either/or—no boundaries at all or to the extreme. Yes?"*

MARCUS: **Yes. So, when we are estranged from our children how do we reconcile the holding of boundaries with a broken heart?**

THEO: *"It is no different. Just because your heart is breaking, you are feeling a heightened emotionality, does not mean one should collapse the boundary or make it stronger. The beingness of everyone, each soul, is understanding that you all deserve respect. You are divine master beings, and the way your world will work for peace is respecting one another. Yes?"*

MARCUS: **Absolutely. So, while we are on this topic, how do we heal a broken heart?**

THEO: *"It is possible, but it is also to notice what you are noticing. What is a broken heart? It is a perception that someone did something to you that disappointed you. So, what is the disappointment and how can that be healed on the inner? Who is disappointed? What part of you has disappointment and sadness? A part of that is grief— grieving for what could have been, the fantasies that one creates for the outcomes it desires."*

MARCUS: Are the kids coming in today older souls, or is this time just like any other time in history?

THEO: *"They are very bright. But understand this: it is all the evolutionary process of expanded consciousness. However, when you label a child by those labels of greatness, that is how people perceive, then there are no boundaries for them. It is a different way of being with them that is a disserve to that child."*

MARCUS: How can we best serve our children, THEO?

THEO: *"By being an example of life in that unconditional loving state. And that is not to excuse bad behavior, it is not to let go of boundaries, but being in that state, living in that state, living who you are and your truths and core values because children are watching. It is not only what you say, it is how you express yourself that they learn from, most importantly."*

When we embrace the reality that we choose our birth family prior to incarnating, that we have soul contracts with one or more of our parents, siblings, children, or spouses (as we discussed in the previous chapter) and that these agreements are entered into for the learning of emotions that each relationship brings, things begin to make a little more sense. It takes the pressure off us feeling that all our family relationships need to be harmonious. Many are just what they are, and you recognize that you are vibrating at different frequencies, each with a different worldview. You don't have to "make anything happen" but can just let them be what they will. Regarding family members, particularly siblings, who you might not be resonating with for whatever reason, we often hear THEO ask, "If you met them today for the first time, would you feel the attraction to have a relationship?" Most often, the answer is no.

In this next conversation with Andrea, THEO shares how we can simultaneously love our kids (or anybody) while not liking their human behavior, and how important it is to remember that no one can make us feel anything—that we feel but are not *made to feel* anything by anyone. To own our feelings such as "I feel when" instead of "you made me feel" has a very different energy. One has a victim feeling—blaming the other, while the other is taking responsibility for our own feelings. Andrea's awareness of this as told in her story reflects how powerful this can be when communicating with your children, ex-spouses, or anyone else you may have conflict with.

THEO LIVE WITH ANDREA

ANDREA: Speaking of obligation and relationships, my daughter and I have been doing this dance for a while, and although I love her dearly, I often feel triggered by her. And when I go on the inner to ask myself, "What is the trigger? Can I love her as she is?" I get this answer that I sense her dad's energy on her, and I am reacting to that energy. Can you assist me in shifting this dynamic?

THEO: *"So, when you recognize it is not her at all, that it is her father's energy that you are feeling, ask yourself 'Who inside of me is reactive to him?'"*

ANDREA: Right. With our kids, and I speak as a mother, I feel responsible for raising them, showing them, guiding them, loving them. There are parts of them sometimes that are hard for me, and I know that I can love them, but I do not like some parts of them.

THEO: *"That is true in human experience. Yes?"*

ANDREA: Yes, but I feel guilty about it because I tell myself I should like them. They are my kids.

THEO: *"Understand this, you love them, you love their souls. You do not have to like what they do all the time, or their personal traits. It is all part of their human experience and growth."*

ANDREA: It is. With that thought, THEO, I have a question about distinguishing and being able to embody the love. We can love their soul and dislike their personality, and when I sit with that,

at times, it is hard for me to separate the two and being able—
when I don't like the personality—to feel the energy or frequency
of loving the soul. It is almost like a rejection. Can you speak
to us a little bit about loving and disliking at the same time?

THEO: *"The loving of a soul is an unconditional state. You are experiencing a reactivity to the human personality. You do not like the action
or the words. So, address it on the inner. What is it you are reactive
to, and is it possibly a teaching for you? Share, 'When this occurred,
this is how I felt.' Identify your own feelings. Most often, it is about
being disrespected, yes?"*

ANDREA: For me, yes.

THEO: *"So, it's a discussion about respect, yes?"*

ANDREA: Yes. It is mostly for me about respect as that is one of my
highest values.

THEO: *"Yes. So, are you respecting them? It goes both ways. Even though
the bodies are younger, that does not mean the soul is. But there
are boundaries to be held about communication—about how things
are said. How time is spent. All those things, yes? But it is about
identifying and owning your feelings and then expressing them. It
is not that you are saying, 'You did this to me,' but rather 'I felt, my
feelings were hurt. You didn't hurt my feelings, but I did feel hurt
by your actions.' So, it is important to understand the intention, and
we know about the most recent experience—the intention was not to
hurt. It was only to be a bit narcissistic. Young people do this. They
are all narcissistic. It is all about them, but that is the growth in the
human experience, isn't it? So, the growth occurs for both when you
speak to the sadness that you felt, and you share this out of love,
which it truly is. 'I love you so much. I love spending time with you. I
was looking forward to being together.'"*

ANDREA: That is exactly what I said the next morning.

THEO: *"Yes, and it was better received then, yes?"*

ANDREA: Yes. She cried all night. I felt it in my soul, in my heart,
that she was so sad.

THEO: *"Her intention wasn't to hurt you at all, but the truth is you both felt sad."*

ANDREA: Yes. Absolutely.

THEO: *"But you felt sad, and the intention wasn't to disrespect you. She just wanted to do what she wanted to do, but you taught her that actions have reactions and consequences and that communication is a great gift you give her for each other."*

ANDREA: Yes. And I felt her shift when I apologized for the way I delivered the message to her. I could feel her body relaxing, so it felt good.

THEO: *"Yes. So, you are a testament to 'It's not what you say, but it is how you say it.'"*

ANDREA: Absolutely, it is. Her father and I have had this tremendous love for each other, but it has shifted. Even though we have triggered each other a lot, I think we mirror to each other some things that we are healing within each of us and growing. As of late, he does not talk to me at all, and when I address it with him—how we have a child together, how it is important for us to talk about her, that she is having some challenges as a teenager—he just chooses not to have anything to do with it. I already set a boundary with him that it is important for me since she is our daughter, and I want him to talk to me. Nothing. It is almost like passive aggressiveness, and I am feeling at a bit of a loss. It is frustrating when someone does not want to talk to you about a child that you have in common, no matter what you do. There is no communication. So, will it be safe for me to say, "We talked about this. You do not want to engage. That is all right," and talk to him on a soul level, and then just work with my daughter and stop pushing him to communicate?

THEO: *"Of course. You cannot make him do what you want him to do. You never could. So, talk soul-to-soul to him. That is the only alternative you have at this point."*

ANDREA: She is old enough where I can work with her directly and not be so worried about the communication with him.

THEO: "Correct. They have a relationship between them, regardless of you, and you are not to be in the middle of it. You address your relationship with her directly."

ANDREA: Thank you, THEO.

ANDREA SHARES HER EXPERIENCE

THEO taught me the importance of loving myself first and acknowledging that what happened in my life in the past (e.g., childhood abuse) happened for me, not to me, breaking a pattern of feeling like a victim. I had felt powerless, which negatively affected my experience in life and in all my relationships.

My relationship with my daughters began shifting dramatically. I have 14-year-old and 7-year-old daughters, and with the help of THEO, I understood that I can love their soul and I don't necessarily need to like their personality or behavioral choices at times. That it is acceptable for me as their mother to dislike their choices and still love them. That realization freed me for many years of feeling guilty for disliking their disrespectful conduct. I learned to set up healthy boundaries and expectations with them, out of love for the self and for them and that my kids needed boundaries to understand how to engage in a healthy manner with me and in their relationships in life. They learned the importance of self-respect and to ask for what they want in a relationship and to hold people accountable. I also learned that I must respect them too to also receive that respect and that just because their body is young does not make them less divine or spiritually masterful to make choices in their lives. THEO's wisdom and practical teachings such as using the "I" statements when addressing a concern with my children (e.g., "I feel unloved when you don't pick up after yourself" puts the ownership of my feelings on me and the message is better received by my daughters.

THEO also taught me to be less reactive with my kids by simply asking myself when I feel triggered, "Who within me is feeling the discomfort?" and to identify early if the trigger was actually created by my daughter, or is it a projection I saw in her from my relationship with her father? That single practice has substantially reduced our disagreements and arguments bringing more peace into our lives.

Our family is stronger and happier today thanks to the up-leveling of our relationship through THEO's loving mentorship.

MARCUS: How can we be more child-like?

THEO: *"By communicating with the fragmented aspects of the soul. What do they want? How do they wish to express? Let them out to play."*

MARCUS: Speak more about that please.

THEO: *"The childlike qualities, a lightness of being, of being fully present in the moment-to-moment life experience as you have an awareness of being a child. If someone said, 'We are leaving in five minutes,' the child thinks that is an eternity, do they not? One minute is an eternity in their life because of extreme full presence in the moment of now. And in that moment of now is truly all you will have, so be fully in it. Yes, you can plan for the future or have ideas and imaginations of creations to come, but draw yourself back to this moment and the experience in it. That is truly living your life fully. And if you are too far in the past, there is recrimination—what could I have done differently? It is reliving the old that is already complete; it is history. Being in the moment-to-moment experience and to notice what you are noticing in that moment allows you to be fully present in life."*

MARCUS: **Please speak more to being present, and to "noticing what we're noticing." Is this a habit we can form?**

THEO: *"It is. Be fully present in any conversation that you are having. Focus is another word for it. If you are eating a meal, how is the food tasting? Most inhale the food and do not even know what it tastes like because they are not present in the experience of it—savoring that expression and experience, whatever it is—whether it is eating or speaking or listening. That is the presence that we are talking about."*

MARCUS: **How do we keep our sense of humor when things get a little tough?**

THEO: *"Look for the humor. It does not matter how dire it is. Is there something humorous within it? Humans are funny in how they express themselves."*

MARCUS: **What do you find funniest about us?**

THEO: *"Everything."*

MARCUS: **Speak more to that.**

THEO: *"You keep repeating patterns that you won't stop. All you must do is to be fully present in your experience, and you can see the humor in almost all conversations and interactions with one another. Human nature has great humor within it."*

MARCUS: **It can be hysterical.**

THEO: *"Yes, or depressive."*

MARCUS: **Right. So, how do we develop one if we feel we do not have a sense of humor?**

THEO: *"Quit taking yourself so seriously. It is very simple."*

MARCUS: **Right. I have heard you say many times that spirit likes fun.**

THEO: *"Spirit does like fun. Think in terms of when you are emotional, whether you are crying or laughing. Either one opens you up. It does not contract you. But laughter is truly opening, isn't it? Your chest, your heart, is open. Your shoulders are dropped and are not in the position of protection and contraction. It is freeing."*

MARCUS: Please speak to the topic of loyalty in our birth family.

THEO: *"Do they deserve it? Loyalty is trust. Trust is not freely given but earned. Have they earned your loyalty, your trust?"*

MARCUS: You have said the same is true for obligation. Please expand upon your suggestion that we ask ourselves, "Are we doing it for love, or are we doing it out of love?"

THEO: *"You answered the question. It is just insight, isn't it? It is the knowledge of the intention behind the action. Are you fulfilling what you deem as an obligation to another, and what is your intention in doing so? If you give to another, what are you going to get back? What is your desired outcome?"*

MARCUS: Speak to us about how to shift the perception of blame to empowerment.

THEO: *"When you quit blaming others and know that you have created in your life opportunities of growth, it gives you that freedom."*

CHAPTER TEN

COMMUNICATION

"The gift you have in your human experience is the ability to communicate. To be a great communicator is to speak your truth."

—THEO

IN HIS BOOK "The Art of Happiness" The Dalai Lama writes, "If you want others to be happy, practice compassion. If you want to be happy, practice compassion." THEO often suggests that when faced with any decision to ask ourselves, "What would love do?" They answer that love would act with compassion. Whenever we have any conflict or discord in our relationship we eventually get to a point (most of the time sooner than later) where we ask ourselves "If I had this to do all over, what could I have done or said to act more compassionately?" Asking this one question resolves conflict quickly and helps to put things back in perspective. Another question that has worked well when each of us desires a different outcome or would prefer not to compromise is "For which one of us is the outcome of this more important?" Typically, that becomes evident early in the discussion and can lead to a peaceful conclusion.

Embracing THEO's teachings on soul integration, understanding why we believe, think, and act the way we do, and how to change unhealthy beliefs and behaviors, can significantly improve our communication skills. One of the fragmented aspects of the soul—the "orphan" as THEO calls it—that affects our ability to communicate peacefully and productively, without taking things personally, is what we call "the falsely accused orphan." That aspect of Self that reacts, sometimes forcefully, when we feel someone is falsely accusing us of anything we feel we did not do or say. Often this reaction can originate from another lifetime where we were persecuted for telling our truth. Or maybe from this lifetime where we spoke our truth but were not believed. This may be an area to explore if you are prone to taking things personally and reacting with anger, rather than responding more as an observer. As the noticer of what is happening in that moment, you may see that whoever you are in conversation with might just be projecting onto you some aspect of themselves that is acting out. Responding with compassion and patience, can be the best way of diffusing an otherwise volatile situation, and it always helps to look at the intention behind anything said that triggers you.

And in all types of relationships there also looms the possibility that we may find ourselves in a conversation where we have a solution to a problem being discussed, whether the other wants to hear about it or not. Most of us are experts at solving others' problems! And most of the time we are also, out of love, desiring to keep them from being hurt or experiencing disappointment—which is quite common for "fixers" and "saviors." But what if their soul desires the learning of doing it on their own? What if they need to experience the pain of doing for themselves to learn compassion and empathy? One of our favorite THEO metaphors is to imagine the butterfly as it begins to emerge from the cocoon. If, as it is struggling to get free, you were to assist it by clipping the cocoon to free it early, it would die for it would not have built the musculature developed in the process of emerging that will be required for it to fly. Where in your life do recognize opportunities to allow your loved ones the opportunity to develop their own musculature?

MARCUS: **THEO, how do we best communicate with those who would judge or criticize us for turning our backs on our religious upbringing to follow a more personally fulfilling spiritual path?**

THEO: *"To remember that it has nothing to do with you. Ultimately, it is all about them, isn't it?"*

MARCUS: **Right.**

THEO: *"It is all about their limiting beliefs, their fears. For anytime there is judgment, it is a projection of one's own fear."*

MARCUS: **And we deal with not being part of the tribe anymore, which can lead to feelings of abandonment.**

THEO: *"Yes. That is where courage comes. To be the authentic self is a* courageous act. It is the path of the hero's walk, for most adhere to the edicts of the structure of the family to belong and to survive in that environment. So, for ones who do step out, it is the mobile effect that we speak about, to take your piece out of that hanging balance of family to become independent of that, which then creates an imbalance within it for a time."

MARCUS: **How do you define the hero's path?**

THEO: "It is courageous to live one's own life to make choices for one's own soul's path regardless of the opinions of others."

MARCUS: **And as we let go of our past, it frees us up to focus on the future.**

THEO: "Yes. And ultimately, you are not letting go of your past. It exists. It is history, but your perceptions have changed about it."

MARCUS: **What do you see as the biggest mistake people make in interacting with one another?**

THEO: "Withholds. Not communicating. Not speaking the truth to one another."

MARCUS: **How can we become better communicators? Do we just flip that?**

THEO: "Yes, just flip it. It does not have to be harsh. Many of you have thought that to speak your truth you have to do it in anger because that is the only time you can be heard, and that is not true. It can be done with kindness and compassion in letting them know what your expectations and desires are. 'This is what is important to me. I feel loved when this or that is done because it is important to me.' Those things, those expectations, cannot be met unless they are voiced because it is inappropriate to assume that another can read your mind, even though you are very sentient beings capable of accessing your intuition and your knowing, with the ability to connect telepathically, and even with those different ways of receiving. You have the gift, and responsibility, of speaking it. And in that speaking, know that communication is not only speaking but listening, listening acutely to another, and honoring them with being heard.

Each person desires to be seen and heard completely and not to feel invalidated when they share how they feel."

MARCUS: So, how do we become better listeners?

THEO: *"Keep your mouth shut, yes?"*

MARCUS: That would be a good start, wouldn't it?

THEO: *"Most often people are responding to another's communication before it is even complete. Your intelligence engages thinking it knows how to respond to a statement that is not even complete. That is a disservice to you both. So, give yourself a few seconds before you respond to be sure you have heard the entire statement. You could even ask. 'Is there more you would like to say before I respond?' That is validating the speaker, but it is also being sure you know the statement you are responding to."*

MARCUS: Speak to the process of showing our emotions while we communicate. Many have been raised that to show emotions is a sign of weakness.

THEO: *"Or even to feel the feelings. It is disservice because what you have come to do on a soul level is to experience feelings and emotions. Yet, they are judged, and people are told they are too emotional if they share their feelings. It is all in the way that you share them, isn't it? If you become hysterical and share feelings only in hysterics, it is off-putting. Then, no one wants to listen to that. It is drama. But if you say, 'I feel' and share that information directly and succinctly and clearly, without judgment and blame, you can be heard even better."*

MARCUS: What would you say to assist those wishing to overcome shyness to become more socially comfortable and to be a better communicator?

THEO: *"They have history of when they have spoken up to be judged by those whom they have been speaking to, so they become wary of sharing and for fear of being harmed."*

MARCUS: And it could very well be an adopted belief from a previous incarnation, correct?

THEO: *"It could be, yes. It is engrained in the soul, and so one keeps quiet. But not sharing your truth, not sharing the words with others, is a disservice to the self and to the world. The gift of your truth is what you bring."*

MARCUS: Speak more to the uniqueness of what we bring.

THEO: *"Each and every one of you is incredibly unique. It is a miracle that you are in your body. There are billions of souls that could have been in your body. But you are in it, and you are a unique divine master being that has chosen this human experience in this time of consciousness shift. And in that, you have a unique tone note that no one else has. Not one person on the planet has it except you. That is how unique you are. We call it the soul note, and it is your expression. You can sing it. You can speak it. You can write it. Whatever it is to share your soul note to the world is that truth that is unique. Others may do things and experience things similarly to you, but they do not have your voice and your sound and your words and your vision. That is unique unto you. So, it has been proven that you each have a unique way of seeing the world or hearing the world or experiencing the world. If there is an accident and there are several people that have observed it, the interviewer can interview each and every one of you, and you will not have the same story because you all see it a little differently. It would be a very boring world if there was only one book written because there is already one book. Someone already did that. Why should you do that? Or one song has been composed and no others because those who would have been composers say, 'That has already been done. Somebody did it.' Nobody can do what you do. They may do something similarly, but they do not have your certain perceptions or your abilities."*

MARCUS: How about when we want to speak, but the words just do not seem to come to us?

THEO: *"There are moments when you should not speak. That is why the words do not come out."*

MARCUS: Speak more to that.

THEO: *"It would not be received, so your soul stops you from speaking. But that is not always."*

MARCUS: **How do we conjure up the courage to speak when we are feeling fearful?**

THEO: *"It is fear-based for the desire to be accepted and loved is so great, you are afraid to speak your truth for the possibility of non-acceptance and abandonment."*

MARCUS: **How do we not take things personally?**

THEO: *"It is difficult in the human experience, and it begins at an early age out of the desire to be loved. So, there is an assumption that if something occurs, it must be one's fault, and then it engages the un-justification of events or the feeling therein."*

MARCUS: **How do we become more emotionally masterful—to be less defensive or reactive?**

THEO: *"Clarify the comments. In your communication, if one is feeling this judgment, clarify what was said, to be sure one is not just assuming what another means. 'This is what I heard you say. Is that correct?,' and then respond. For most times, there is not an intention to harm."*

MARCUS: **Or to accuse?**

THEO: *"Or to accuse."*

MARCUS: **I have heard you speak about the falsely accused orphan or fragmented aspect of the soul. Talk to us about working with that falsely accused part of self.**

THEO: *"Everybody has that. Every human has it. A core value in human experience for most, not all, but most, is the value of truth. So, ultimately, when someone is feeling accused and the truth is that one has done nothing, there is a reaction to it because it goes to the undermining of one's core value that they are truthful."*

MARCUS: **It feels like an attack on our integrity.**

THEO: *"Yes, isn't truth a part of integrity? What is integrity? Being integrated in your being."*

MARCUS: **From my personal experience, I have noticed that the falsely accused orphan was created in a previous incarnation** where I know of having been falsely accused or persecuted for telling my truth in that lifetime. Talk to us about accessing the feeling of that, even if there is not a specific age or circumference that we can attach to it.

THEO: "There is a knowing, and the reactivity is so strong because of the fear of persecution or harm . . . misjudged . . . and in the past, in other times, you call the past. In multidimensional experiences, there has been persecution, even death. Even today, it occurs. There are those falsely accused who are put to death. So, it is not just in previous centuries or times in the human experience upon this planet; it has been a continuum."

MARCUS: Help us to respond, as opposed to react, to being falsely accused.

THEO: "That is a trigger for many, many people to be blamed for something that is not in your purview. It is not yours to carry. So, the response would be clearly, 'No, I did not do that.' You can stand firm in the truth of your being. The accuser may be reacting to a belief formed in a previous incarnation or in this incarnation possibly. It has to do with blame."

MARCUS: Speak more to that.

THEO: "Most injustices are beings blaming others for something they perceive as happening to them or done to them. We invite you to notice what you are noticing. Are you reactive? Why are you reactive? Who inside of you has the anger?"

MARCUS: That inside-out job again.

THEO: "Yes."

MARCUS: Let's talk about anger and its appropriate use.

THEO: "It does not have to be detrimental. It can be motivational, yes?"

MARCUS: Yes. Speak more to that.

THEO: "So, if something has been a repetitive pattern or if there is procrastination and it builds up to chaos, that exhibits in anger at the self for not doing. It motivates you to do, doesn't it?"

MARCUS: Yes, it can be very motivating.

THEO: "Anger can propel you forward in speaking your truth as well. It is when something intolerable has happened, and you speak out about it."

MARCUS: How can we express anger without it creating more stress in our body?

THEO: "Most often, what is underlying anger is sadness, and anger can cover over sadness that is uncomfortable."

MARCUS: How do we know when that is the situation?

THEO: "By self-examination."

MARCUS: What do you mean when you talk about "holding state" for people when we observe them being emotionally triggered and reactive?

THEO: "Not being reactive to their emotional breakdown, you might say. Is it about you? No, it is about whatever is triggering them and what they are reactive to. So, if you are taking it on as your own, why would you do that?"

MARCUS: It is not our stuff anyway.

THEO: "No. So, if you know that, you can stand steadfast in support of one who is in chaos at that moment."

MARCUS: Energetically, how do we do that?

THEO: "When you know that it does not have anything to do with you, it is easy to do."

MARCUS: Just love on them?

THEO: "Correct, what would love do?"

MARCUS: It is a good fallback, isn't it?

THEO: "It is, yes."

MARCUS: It seems that when you say "Notice what you are noticing," you are talking about awareness and observation.

THEO: "Many teachings, yes. It is awareness, isn't it? Being aware. Being awake in life. Observing yourself and things around you."

MARCUS: What more is there to share about transforming conflict into a peaceful resolution?

THEO: *"Acknowledge that it is there. Do not try to stop it. Don't invalidate another."*

MARCUS: Validation is a powerful thing.

THEO: *"The power of validation is something that one feels when they feel heard. For an example, you are expressing 'I feel' in whatever it is to someone, and they say, 'No, you don't. You do not feel that. You feel this way.' That is an invalidation of the person's truth and their feelings and their expression. They feel unheard, which invalidates them even further to feeling unseen."*

MARCUS: What are the best ways we can validate others?

THEO: *"Listening acutely and not responding before the statement is finished. Listen and then check with the individual. 'Have I heard everything? This is what I heard.' Give feedback to them of what you heard them say. 'Is that correct?' And then respond. For most often, you are responding before you have heard. That is an invalidation as well."*

MARCUS: Our mind starts firing, and we are no longer listening.

THEO: *"Correct. You are only listening to your own thoughts that you think are better, yes? 'My idea is better than yours,' so to speak."*

The following dialogue between Maria and THEO reminds us how often two people enter a relationship bringing with them beliefs that were formed early in life that created volatility and poor communication skills in their adult lives. We wonder how many marriages end because they never learn to communicate and take responsibility for their own emotional growth, even though there is great love between them. These beliefs can often lead to feelings of woundedness that set the stage for the old paradigm in romantic relationships: you fill the woundedness in me, and I'll fill it in you. It rarely works out. One of the heartening aspects of Maria's story is how willing her husband, who was not present for this conversation, was to embrace this new way of communicating.

THEO LIVE WITH MARIA

MARIA: I notice patterns of behavior with my husband. They can be volatile, and when we are both in that state, we cannot really help each other. There are periods where there is presence and where we can communicate heart-to-heart. We have a 4-year-old daughter. I want to make sure I am doing what is best for her. I would like to know if I should trust in this relationship since I can see the progress. I do see where it can be a benefit for all of us and we can help each other, but there are times I see where it is not so great. Do you have any clarity for me?

THEO: "It is important for you to change your interactions with each other. You are both very reactive, and it is what we call the orphanage, the fragmented aspects of your soul that act out and become emotionally volatile. So, it is to have a willingness to do that inner work to wholeness within the self which leads to non-reactivity. So, the woundedness in you attracted the woundedness in him and for you to take care of him. And you had an expectation that he will take care of you. It is impossible. It does not mean you are bad people. It is just you are wounded. It is these little ones that you just connected to that oversee your emotional reactivity. So, when they become fearful, that is when it gets out of control and reactive, yes?"

MARIA: Yes.

THEO: "So, you sit down and have a meeting, and how you can do that is not doing it for each other but doing it for yourselves. 'I noticed that I react. It is not the adult me, but I am working on having an awareness, and this is what I am going to do. Are you willing to do the same?' It is a contract you make with each other. There is love there, but these little fragmented aspects of both your souls are in charge. It is like the kindergartener having no teacher, and everybody is *running around screaming. It can work, but you both must be willing to change. Identify on the inner, and recognize where you have come from. You both came from environments that were volatile, and so, to some extent, there is a belief in that volatility is passion. It has a certain passion, and it does. But not the kind that you want to live with, but that has been construed as love, yes?"*

MARIA: Yes, that is the only love I understood for a long time.

THEO: *"Of course. And he, as well. So, you were a perfect match for that, but not for your lifetime."*

MARIA: No.

THEO: *"There can be a dialog, a conversation. 'This is what we can change. It does not have to be this way,' and it doesn't, if both are willing to do the inner work of change and not to be afraid of it. So, ask him if he is willing."*

MARIA: Okay.

THEO: *"He doesn't like it any better than you do."*

MARIA: We both are willing.

THEO: *"And you both have the desire for your child to have something better."*

MARIA: Yes. That is the biggest desire.

THEO: *"Good. So, you agree."*

MARIA: Yes.

THEO: *"You can make it work, and he wants happiness just as much as you do because you have a good foundation for that. We don't say that to everybody."*

MARIA: I appreciate that because my intuition tells me that is true. I just needed to hear it from you.

THEO: *"It is true, but you have to have a realistic discussion about it and not in a volatile time. When you have disagreements, do not let them get out of control, and how you can do that is have a word you can say to each other that stops the spiraling out of control. Just decide on a word together. It might be a funny word that stops it."*

MARIA: I was just thinking about that. I was going to say a funny word.

THEO: "It will snap you both out of the energy. And if it is a necessity to have a dialogue about something that you are arguing about, take a break, take time, and come back to it at a non-volatile time, so the ears will be open to hear and there is no reaction, yes?"

MARIA: Yes. Okay. Thank you.

THEO: "Good. You feel better, don't you?"

MARIA: So much better.

THEO: "We can see you are not shaking."

MARIA: I am not. I feel healed.

THEO: "Good."

MARIA SHARES HER EXPERIENCE

When you are codependent, your world is limited. When you are free from that bondage, life is limitless. Thanks to the message I received from THEO, the confirmation that my husband and I both want the same thing gave me hope and reaffirmed my inner knowing. This process enlightened me.

I have always wished to give my daughter everything that I always wanted as a child, a happy upbringing with healthy relationships. Now more so than ever, I know that I can give this gift to her and to myself. It is a relief to know that my husband and I can and will make it work. Through the process shared by THEO, we can work through our reactivity and improve our communication.

Since my conversation with THEO, my husband and I have been more compassionate and understanding of one another. We have both grown tremendously and are building the life that we want. This is priceless. The best part is that my daughter gets to witness this transformation. We all are learning and growing together.

MARCUS: **How would you suggest we respond to a situation where there are two or more people in collusion?**

THEO: *"Step away from it. Don't get involved because there are those that wish others to agree with their point of view. They enlist them to agree with them, to be part of their team in judging someone else. Hold your own counsel. Hold your own truth and speak it."*

MARCUS: **Talk to us about the power of soul-to-soul communication when we are unable to achieve results communicating in the physical.**

THEO: *"When the ears cannot hear. When there is the inability to speak to someone who cannot hear you, the soul is always listening. So, the soul of you can speak to the soul of that individual directly, connecting heart to heart and soul to soul."*

MARCUS: **That can move mountains in the physical?**

THEO: *"It can."*

MARCUS: **It has that much power?**

THEO: *"It does, and most importantly, when it is soul-to-soul communication, heart to heart, then whatever is the resolution or the information that comes into that heart informs the mind, and the mind thinks whatever they are doing or whatever is happening is their idea. And they can believe in that. Yes?"*

MARCUS: **Yes. Please speak to the power and process of disentanglement.**

THEO: *"It is all energy. Disentanglement is energy disentangling where the individual gives their power to another to be accepted or loved, and the other does the same in return. So, you are giving your power away to each other. So, disentanglement can be that you speak clearly that 'I give back to you all your power you have given to me over time in all multidimensional experiences, and I give it back to you with love. And I (give your name) take back my power from you that I have given over time in all multidimensional experiences and I take my power back from you with love now.' Always with love."*

MARCUS: **Is there an energetic disconnect that takes place?**

THEO: *"Yes."*

MARCUS: **You have spoken about cutting the psychic cord.**

THEO: *"Here, too, that you are psychically attached to each other. It is like a woven rope. You can see it as a golden energy cord, and it is attached to a part of your body. You will know where you have the attachment with others, and you can sever it. You can cut it, just as you would when surgically cutting the cord—an umbilical cord."*

MARCUS: **And does that detach that person from us psychically?**

THEO: *"It does. But dependent upon how much you have been engaged in, you may need to do it more than once. And know this: it is an energy shift that occurs, and so that individual may contact you because they feel the energy shift."*

MARCUS: **Does the disentanglement process also work to detach from circumstances or conditions?**

THEO: *"Those are usually perpetuated by people, aren't they?"*

MARCUS: **Right, and they are usually perpetuated by beliefs, too, yes?**

THEO: *"Yes. And perceptions."*

MARCUS: **So, maybe we are talking about disentangling from old beliefs.**

THEO: *"You are doing that with rewriting the script."*

MARCUS: **Let's talk more about rewriting the script. You speak about this often.**

THEO: *"We do. So, you have been living in a script. You are living in your own film, your own theater, and you have control of how it is lived—how you act as the character in it, as the star. What are the words you want to say? What are the things that you know? What are the changes that have happened so that the old script no longer serves you? It is self-speak. How do you talk to yourself? When you learn how to love the self unconditionally, your self-speak is encouraging, not discouraging. That is the rewriting of the script. That was then, this is now. 'This is what I have learned and benefited by my experiences of the past, and this is what I have learned, and this is who I am today.'"*

MARCUS: **So, we rewrite that script and yet there is some part of our self that just does not believe it.**

THEO: *"Then you are stuck in the old paradigm because you must believe it to live it."*

MARCUS: **So, we just must go inside and figure out which aspect of our self does not believe it.**

THEO: *"Yes. Because the strength of your beliefs is what controls your life."*

MARCUS: **THEO, is there anything else to say about being a great communicator that I have not asked?**

THEO: *"Know it goes both ways—acute listening and truthful speaking.*

Just a single moment of revelation can change every communication that follows—that one moment when we become aware of why we do or say something that may hurt other's feelings or cause disharmony in a relationship. How many times do we snap for no reason or say something—unconsciously, it's just how we say things—that don't carry the intention we were feeling, yet come across as critical or harsh? We find just this dynamic in Ole's session with THEO and in the moment of awareness that it was a 42-year-old aspect of himself feeling jealousy towards his wife, everything changes. It is also interesting that these fragmented aspects create beliefs about our ourselves that drive our emotional reactivity and are not always created in our early years, as we see here. And as you read Ole's story following the session, you will notice something very interesting about how his wife, Vicky, is now responding to him.

THEO LIVE WITH OLE

OLE: I find myself now and then snapping at my wife for no reason, and I cannot explain why that is. And when I do it, I feel so bad.

THEO: "So, that is a reaction to certain stimulus that occurs. That is a moment that you can connect to that part of self that is reactive for a greater understanding. So, now you have an awareness that you can ask who it is and how old they are to get some clarity. So, you can close your eyes now in the remembrance of that reaction, for you are feeling it in your body, are you not?"

OLE: Yes, I am.

THEO: "So, go into the breath and into the feeling in the body, for that will be your path to this discovery. So, breathe. Ask, 'Who inside is uncomfortable? How old is he?'"

OLE: What I see right now is that I lived there at home in Denmark until I was 42, and then went to the States and got married. What I see is myself on the last evening being at home with my mom and dad, giving my dad a present, and my dad being sad that I am leaving. I hadn't even realized until recently that when I left them after 42 years, I gave up all of my friends and family—not given up—but I used to seeing them every day, and I don't do that anymore. When I left home, all I had was a phone and occasional visits.

THEO: "So, how old is he?"

OLE: 42.

THEO: "So, you can communicate to him about this. So, he feels sad and abandoned. It does not matter if he is young or older. It is all from the emotional body. You are connected to him."

OLE: Yes, I am.

THEO: "So, now you establish how good it is to be you at this stage in your life, and how he assisted you to have this good life—his strengths. And you will not abandon him. He does not need to feel alone. You will always be with him and support him, and you *appreciate his strengths. Breathe. So, he is giving you the memory of the night before you left."*

OLE: Yes.

THEO: *"You have the realization of the sadness that he has about leaving the family and how sad they were."*

OLE: Yes. When I lived there, I did not have that feeling until I got married, but I feel I am still connected to me from that time.

THEO: *"Excellent. So, ask him why he is reactive in that manner to your wife."*

OLE: He tells me it is jealousy because "she took me away from them."

THEO: *"Yes. It is a revelation, isn't it?"*

OLE: Yes, it is.

THEO: *"So, let him know he doesn't have to be angry at her. She loves him as well. And it was appropriate for you both to come into this life that you have built. And you will always listen to him and hear him. He can be kind to her because you will not abandon him. How does he feel?"*

OLE: He feels relieved and understands.

THEO: *"It is important for you to let him know that it was a natural thing to move and to start one's own life, and the relationship with the father and the love of the father is always with you. It lives inside of you, in both of you, and that is a blessing and a gift."*

OLE: I feel that he can see that I have enough love for both him and my wife, so there is no reason for him to be afraid, that he has a good life, and I have love for him as well.

THEO: *"Yes. So, when you begin to feel that reaction you can support him and let him know, 'I hear you, I love you, and I will not abandon you.'"*

OLE: And he understands that.

THEO: *"So, now you have that tool. And ask him if he would like to come into this life now with you in the strength of that."*

OLE: I hear, yes.

THEO: *"And that you can do it together with love."*

OLE: Yes.

THEO: *"And when you are ready you can open your eyes. Ask him if it is all right to leave at this time. You will come back and talk with him again. You will always be connected, and when you ask him, what is his response?"*

OLE: I got a "Yes," and "Yes" to we will talk again.

THEO: *"And when you are ready you can open your eyes and come back to this moment."*

OLE: Thank you, THEO. I totally appreciate it.

OLE SHARES HIS EXPERIENCE

Since the session with THEO, I have not snapped at Vicky, and our communication and relationship is freer. I am, more than before, looking forward for our future and adventures together.

My wife can feel a difference in our relationship as well. The other night I said something which she normally would perceive as criticism, and she noticed that despite the familiar statement, she felt no criticism. Was it because it was not sent as criticism or because she was consciously no longer receiving it as criticism after my sharing this new awareness? The beautiful thing was that my statement did not carry the underlying energy of criticism. That is quite a change.

The guidance I received from THEO showed me that what triggered me to flare up for no reason was an orphan who felt alone and abandoned and that the problem can be solved with soul integration. I also learned that when something important or big is going to take place in my life, it would be good to consciously tell myself about the decision I have made or action I am going to take and why it is important so that I can soothe that part of self that otherwise might have become reactive.

CHAPTER ELEVEN

LIVING WITH PURPOSE AND PASSION

"Life itself is to be lived with purpose and passion. That is the point, is it not? Manifesting your passion comes from the inner to the outer."

—THEO

ACCORDING TO LEGEND, the Spanish Conquistador Cortez gave his soldiers the order to "burn the boats" as they began their conquest of the Aztecs in 1519. Facing an army much larger than his own, he wanted his men to realize that they had no opportunity to retreat, so they had to give this fight everything they had. Failure was no longer an option and winning this battle became imperative. When manifesting your passion professionally, this can be a great strategy—OR NOT! In many situations, as THEO describes here, it may be wiser to "build a bridge" instead of burning your boats. To do the things necessary to bridge into your dream financially while still working your current job, leading to that day when the pendulum swings in such a way that it will be time, without undue stress, without doubt, to make the move and then burn your boats, but not your bridges! To be clear, we are not mixing metaphors here. Burning your boats does not mean burning your bridges. Following the golden rule and treating everyone with kindness and respect up and down the ladder of your life keep you aligned with your core values. Remember, you are going to encounter the same people on the way down as did on the way up!

When faced with the decision to build the bridge or burn the boats, your greatest asset will be your intuition. Your higher power knows which path is correct for you, so just ask, then listen, and pay attention to what messages you receive. And be intentional in your meditation by asking "Which is the best path for my highest good now?" This is precisely what I did several years ago when I was deciding whether to close my 25-year consulting business and join The THEO Group full-time as Sheila's partner. Just beginning a meditation on a Saturday morning in December of 2014, I asked this very question and immediately saw a vision of burning boats—three big pirate ships on fire—and had no doubt. I knew the story of Cortez, and the message could not have been any clearer. Like THEO says, "In the asking, it is given."

MARCUS: **How do we find our purpose and passion?**

THEO: *"Your purpose is being incarnate—to be alive. That is a purposeful expression of who you are energetically. Passion is how you want to exchange your energy in your life, your human experience upon this planet, being passionate about what you do, your actions being taken, and what you learn."*

MARCUS: **Is it true that if we do what makes us happy, the money will follow?**

THEO: *"Yes. But many cannot believe it because you do not allow yourself to do what makes you happy. Most know when they are young that they have chosen to come into this lifetime to be significant. Significance comes from expressing your energy in a way that has passion in it. However, in the human experience, as you grow, there are those that visit upon you their judgments and their perceptions of who or what you should do or be, and humans accept that from the outer experience to survive. They give their authority, or power, as you speak of it, over to another because their opinions are so important for survival sake that one adopts beliefs about the self that are simply untrue."*

MARCUS: **What do you say to people that cannot seem to discover their passion?**

THEO: *"They are afraid to claim it. Under the 'I don't know' is the knowing. But because one has disempowered the self so much by adopting untrue beliefs of themselves, they feel they cannot choose what they would love."*

MARCUS: **How do we find what we love?**

THEO: *"Go on the inner. The inner being of you knows. What would you do if you had all you needed, and conditions and circumstances did not matter? You have everything that you need, all the resources. What would you do? Because most of the time you think in terms of 'I must have before I can do,' and in this, you limit yourself. So, you say to yourself, 'I can't do that because I don't have this or that,' and so then you cannot even dream what it would be. You cannot even envision or imagine it because that limiting thought is so deeply ingrained."*

MARCUS: It sounds like we just must decide for it. What happens then, THEO, when a decision gets made?

THEO: *"The universal energy, the quantum field, the energy that is ever-present around you aligns with that decision, making it a must, to bring you resources, the things that you need, to move in the direction of the outcome you desire."*

MARCUS: How do we know if we are in alignment with our soul's purpose for incarnating?

THEO: *"You know how it feels. If you are not in alignment, you do not feel energetically aligned in your body. You feel out of balance . . . out of sorts are words we hear . . . even depressed."*

MARCUS: What is the most important thing that we need to know to be genuinely happy in our profession?

THEO: *"Being aware of what your gifts are. Be in an environment in which you can be expressing the gifts that you have—and you all have them that are innate in you—including things that you also learned and educated yourself with, whether it is in a formal education or simply living. Life is an education as well. What do you do that you are compelled to do? That informs you. If you are an artist, you sit at your desk, and you make pictures as you talk to someone. You are compelled to do creative expression, whether you are doing it for a business or not. The things you do that you are interested in, that you read about, that you want to absorb are the things that are informing you of what you love. You are not unconscious to that because your soul draws you down that path to do them no matter what."*

MARCUS: How do we conjure the courage to make the change necessary when we are in an unhappy situation professionally?

THEO: *"Most think, in personal and professional relationships, 'If I release this one, there may not be another. How will I survive?' You are the* creator of that. Create in your being the perfect position. There are people looking for you that will invite you to express your genius. Express your genius! Each of you has a unique expression to give the world. Trust that. What is yours?"

MARCUS: **How do we tap into that?**

THEO: "Just as we have been speaking. What are you interested in? What are you compelled to do? What do you do when you have time to do it? How do you express your energy, and what are you drawn to do? What are you curious about? This informs you of those things. The soul draws to you perfectly what is appropriate for your growth, and it inspires you to look, to see, and to listen, to find out more about certain things of curiosity and interest. Where do you spend your time when not working? Again, you are inspired from the inner to the outer—your imagination. Remember, that as a child, your imagination was so strong you could envision yourself being and doing everything that you were interested in."

MARCUS: **Was Joseph Campbell right, THEO, that we should follow our bliss?**

THEO: "Yes. For anything else, one is marking time unsatisfactorily, and then there is agitation and imbalance that occurs from that. Be aware of your core values as well. What is important to you? What are the things that are most important to you? What do you value most in your relationships and in yourself? Integrity, truth, love, fun . . . all these words are significant in recognizing your core values because the core values that you have of how you live your life is expressed in everything that you do."

MARCUS: **I have heard you say many times that we do not hang up our soul when we go to work.**

THEO: "What we talk about is that everything is spiritual. It is all soul driven. You do not put your soul in the closet where you hang your clothes or your coat and leave it there when you go to the workplace. It is always with you and always expressing through you and to you; for everything you do in every interaction and everything that is in life is soul connected."

MARCUS: **How do we best "win friends and influence people" in the workplace, THEO?**

THEO: *"By being who you are. Be sure you are living in your authenticity. That you are speaking your truth. You are an integrated being. Others wish to be around you because the energy that you are emitting is validating and finding value in others, not only in yourself, and speaking about that. That is the blessing of the interaction that you have with each other—is to see the value in another as you see it in yourself—loving the self and loving others as the self."*

MARCUS: **The Golden Rule.**

THEO: *"It has been around for the entirety of the human experience, and the reason it has is because it's true."*

MARCUS: **What do you see as the new paradigm in leadership?**

THEO: *"Compassion. Many think compassion and sympathy are the same thing. They are not. Compassion has empathy in it, an understanding of another's position and their challenges. It is not excusing bad behavior or giving in or relinquishing boundaries. It is holding boundaries. Having a structure. Having a foundation. A leader inspires. A leader notices the gifts in another and brings them out."*

MARCUS: **What makes a great team player?**

THEO: *"Communication. Communication is extremely important, and not demeaning another. If there are difficulties or something has happened, acknowledge the good in all the things that are and what then can be changed to make it better. So, it is always bringing forth positive energy. Good feedback is positive feedback, and even when something is not working properly to look for the good and change that which needs to be changed. It is only feedback, isn't it? But it is not making another wrong if something is not working properly. Ask 'What can we do to make it work?'"*

MARCUS: **How do you suggest we respond to office gossip and politics?**

THEO: *"That is collusion. There are those who wish to enlist collusion and undermine the foundation. Bring forth a positive. Break that mindset. What we mean by that is have a pattern interrupt in it."*

MARCUS: **Speak more to the pattern interrupt.**

THEO: *"When there is collusion, there needs to be a pattern interrupt in it. For an example, there are those that are colluding, and it is mostly in a negative bent, talking about all the things that are wrong. So, one could ask, 'Well, what are you going to do about it?' because the story is not changing. The story needs to change, so interjecting a question can be a pattern interrupt. 'Is that true? How do you know that? What are you going to do about it?' It interrupts the pattern of the story that is repetitive."*

MARCUS: **How would you recommend that we deal with a difficult boss or manager?**

THEO: *"Holding your boundaries. Communicate. Ask questions. If someone is in an authoritative position, that is difficult, isn't it?"*

MARCUS: **It can be difficult.**

THEO: *"So, either you find a way to interact or you move . . . change. You deserve respect."*

MARCUS: **I think a change typically comes when we realize that we are in an environment that is not aligned with our core values.**

THEO: *"That is correct."*

Alignment with core values is the foundation for all our relationships, personally and professionally. A misalignment of core values in the workplace makes for a very unfulfilling experience. As THEO said, "Everything is spiritual; it is all soul driven." At its foundation, soul integration empowers us to become soul-centered, centered in self, to be the calm in the eye of the storm when necessary (not to be confused with being self-centered). Most workplaces provide us with an abundance of opportunities to observe others as they are emotionally triggered, and as THEO mentions in this conversation with Lydia, being the "fixer" is not our job. Observing, "holding state" energetically, and responding with compassion and empathy is often all we need to do. Allowing each person their own opportunities of growth, and to remember, as we stated earlier, that each person we encounter is in our lives for a reason, a season, or a lifetime.

THEO LIVE WITH LYDIA

LYDIA: THEO, today I would like your help to better understand what is the energy that comes together in a workplace. I know people come together on a mental level to achieve a goal, a vision, in an organizational structure, but is there a calling together on an emotional level as well? And what does that look like?

THEO: "There is a gathering, for as you have heard us state before, groups come together for a purpose, not only for one but for the greater many, as one may say, or the group itself. So, each has an individual opportunity for growth, but then there is the collective energy as well."

LYDIA: Sometimes groups come together, and they are collaborative and co-creative. And you can see the creative energy flowing, but sometimes they are not. Right now, I am struggling to reconcile the positive relationships that I have with my peer colleagues at work with the ongoing challenges and problems with my boss who is somewhat sociopathic. I don't really feel I want to leave, but I feel a knot in my heart and my gut dealing with her. And it ebbs and flows. There are times when I feel empowered, and I feel aligned and authentic. But that always seems to pass, and ultimately that sense of learned helplessness returns. Can you give me some guidance?

THEO: "It is in this that each has their own interaction with her that *has some similar energy to it, as you know. And so, the common denominator of the discord is that this one person, as you can see, is keeping a bit a chaotic energy going because that is what she likes in that sense of control of others."*

LYDIA: She seems to have a lot of credibility though in the hierarchical order, and those of us who struggle to deal with the chaotic energy feel . . . I think that is where the learned helplessness comes in. When she is challenged, she makes little adjustments for a few days or weeks, and then it goes back. I find it hard to stand in my centered space. What advice do you have for me and even for my colleagues?

THEO: *"So, with the personality disorder of sociopathic behaviors keeping people off balance, it allows them to feel that they are controlling everything and everyone, and in the hierarchy, she gives them what they want in the sense she speaks to them and tells them what they want to hear. And so they think everything is fine. Do you understand?"*

LYDIA: Yes. We are just perplexed because we don't know why it is not seen. As we have spoken of, we have called it out, and yet, it does not seem to resonate with our CEO or with some of the other senior leaders that there is a problem here. We are asking for help.

THEO: *"In your own statement, she adjusts when that calling out at work has occurred, an adjustment for them to see that everything has been taken care of and then the reversion back to the old way of being. Sociopaths like the game and the chaos, and so that is what is so off-putting energetically to you and others. You can feel that in your body, as well as observe it in the environment."*

LYDIA: Yes, that would be the knot that I feel in my heart and gut when I must deal with it.

THEO: *"And, the other comment we could make is that with a sociopathic person and their manipulations, let's say, one could say, 'If everything is so good, why do I feel so bad?' because it is that underlying current of manipulation and sowing the seeds of chaos that keeps you all on edge."*

LYDIA: So, THEO, you have talked often that the experience cannot be changed, but how we stand in relation to it can. So, in my standing in relationship to this situation, is there an aspect within me that is reacting? Because it feels to me that in order to just say, "This is what is happening, and this is the energy that is confronting," how do I stand in greater clarity to it? And how do I look within myself so that I am not as triggered or reactive to that person's behavior?

THEO: *"This is so off-putting to you because you're straightforward and you like the truth. It goes against all your core values, and so, that underlying malaise that you feel is because of that. It is not a vibrational match. But, as we have been speaking about, an opportunity will present itself for her to leave, and the energy will shift and change, for which you would be incredibly happy."*

LYDIA: As I was pondering this, THEO, I felt with myself as if there is a part of me that reacts because I have a part of self that thinks it is my responsibility to fix broken relationships or fix it when there is a disconnect between myself and another. Part of me seems to think that it is my responsibility to bear the burden of making the situation work. Please speak to that for me.

THEO: *"The fixer in you? There is a desire for harmony, and one of your primary values in life is to be harmonious. What we can say to this is she cannot allow it, and it is not yours to fix ultimately. Know each one of you is there for your own learning, but it is individually to be fixed within each one. Yes?"*

LYDIA: Yes, I see that.

THEO: *"She is unfixable."*

LYDIA: That is true. I can understand that is her soul's experience. Is there an age of this fixer part of self? Can you help me identify what age that aspect is within me so I can learn to converse with her?

THEO: "When you were very young, you were the warrior."

LYDIA: Even to this day sometimes, yes.

THEO: "Yes, protecting your siblings. So, it started at a young age that there was this warrior part of self that is part of the fixer, you see, carrying the shield and the sword to fight injustice."

LYDIA: This is so helpful. How can I converse with this part of self to say, "I don't need to be the fixer?" How can I be with this process and this experience and hold myself sacred even amidst this engagement with this person?

THEO: "So, when there are those moments where there is extreme discomfort for you, you can then soothe that part of self in that moment internally and speak to her. 'There is nothing to fix here.' That can give you some release and relief. But there is a belief that you are all doing your jobs, and it makes her look good."

LYDIA: Absolutely! She takes all the credit, and I am okay with that because I want to do a good job. It is just unfortunate that all of us doing a good job covers up her problems.

THEO: "So, in the best of all possible circumstances, there is a team working together that the leader gives credit where credit is due. A sociopath does not do this.

LYDIA: THEO, why does she not want to give resources? It harms our ability to be effective or as effective as we could be.

THEO: "So, she thinks of that money as her own, and it is not."

LYDIA: It is not her own, but that is why she does not want to spend it.

THEO: "And she thinks it makes her look better as a leader."

LYDIA: Okay. Is there any way to make a case around that? Is there a way in conversations that I know are going to be upcoming where we are going to be asking for something that we need to do our work for the rest of the year? Is there a way to sidestep that so she will be more receptive to our request?

THEO: "So, it is to present it in the way to be assumptive that you are going to get it, so it is not asking for in essence."

LYDIA: Okay. That is good.

THEO: *"So, in that way, this is what is needed in this business. It is 'I don't need it.'"*

LYDIA: Right. This is what the company needs.

THEO: *"Yes. These are the resources that the company needs to provide the service it provides."*

LYDIA: Is there anything else about my relationships in this workplace that would be helpful for me to know as I go forward in this environment?

THEO: *"What you will find are the relationships that are congenial and friendly, but they do not have the depth of relationship in the sense of soul family."*

LYDIA: That is true.

THEO: *"It is good that they are congenial relationships in the environment, and if another opportunity presents to you that is of great interest, you will not feel that you must stay where you are if you so choose to change because of the relationships. Do you understand?"*

LYDIA: Yes.

THEO: *"So, that gives you some freedom."*

LYDIA: Yes. I could move on to another environment at this time if the opportunity presents itself.

THEO: *"Yes. So, you will have a choice as well. We see this one, of which you have been speaking, is coming to a completion in that environment."*

LYDIA: Okay. And then there will be opportunities for me as well?

THEO: *"Yes. The hierarchy is seeing through the façade to some degree."*

LYDIA: Okay. THEO, thank you for this time. Is there anything else that you wish to leave me with on this subject or any other?

THEO: *"This is a time of grand change on all levels, and see the similarities that are permeating one's own life path—a recognition of core values and standing firm in that soul's essence of one's being, and being deeply rooted in it, not having to fix everything—but living one's own expression through the process as a participant and as a divine master being. You are complete with your asking?"*

LYDIA: I am. Thank you, THEO.

THEO: *"We assist your path. In your asking, it is given. God's love unto you."*

LYDIA SHARES HER EXPERIENCE

My session with THEO on the Art of Relationship at work was immensely helpful and ended up having long-lasting reso-nance. On one level, the information on navigating a difficult boss and the characteristics of that individual helped me in my workplace to stand more effectively in my own authenticity while with her. As a result of my own inner clarity and bound-aries, my interactions with her improved significantly. For example, the guidance to present information and requests assumptively was advice I was able to use very effectively to get buy-in for a resource we needed.

On a second level, the discussion with THEO about the warrior part of self who wants to fix things for others led to increased awareness of how to respond internally to that orphan self and nurture her when she is triggered. With that insight came the realization that true respect and gratitude for others allows them to have their own journey and that their challenges are theirs to fix and not mine to try to ame-liorate for the sake of harmony. Instead, when I am aligned within myself with my own sense of harmony, I am a better contributor and less swayed by the strong emotions of others. This mentoring was valuable in creating a new way of being when working with my colleagues.

And third, on a macro level, THEO's opening guidance about how people come together for a purpose of partici-pating in opportunities for individual and collective growth, coupled with the reminder that while congenial work col-leagues are lovely relationships to have, they may not be soul family, was instrumental to review as I began exploring a new work opportunity. This allowed me to stand aside from the human connections of appreciation and enjoyment I felt for those colleagues and let go of that emotion. The letting go of that personal emotional attachment opened the path of acceptance for me to explore a new potential constellation of creativity and expansion in a new environment. Knowing that a new collaboration is an opportunity of growth not just for me but for all involved is very invigorating and inspiring. THEO's mentoring about everything, and especially the art of relationships in every dimension of experience is so rich and multilayered. I am sure I will be able go back to this session again, and receive even more wisdom.

MARCUS: How do you recommend we participate and contribute to creating the most positive culture wherever we are?

THEO: "Being positive."

MARCUS: It is simple, isn't it?

THEO: "It is. Life can be simple, but humans like to complicate it, don't they?"

MARCUS: Why do you think that is?

THEO: "The intellectual mind is there to problem solve, so what happens is individuals create problems to be solved."

MARCUS: It is just the way the mind works?

THEO: "Yes. Or how life works. But it is also how beliefs dictate the beliefs about self which dictate the outer circumstances. If one does not feel deserving or worthy, there are repetitive patterns that are created to reaffirm that repeatedly, until that pattern and that belief is changed on the inner."

MARCUS: What do you say to people that do not feel like they are expressing their spirituality in the workplace?

THEO: *"What do you want to do? What would give you more satisfaction? If you want more of something, what is the more that you wish and desire?"*

MARCUS: Speak to us about building a bridge from where we are currently to where we really desire to be to express our soul's purpose and to pursue our dreams professionally.

THEO: *"Begin now with what you have. You have much more than you think you do. Most stop because they think they do not have enough money. They do not have enough resources. They do not have this or that. But there are things you can do now to move you in the direction of that outcome that you desire. You do not have to have everything to begin. You can do incremental steps of that to accomplish the larger goal that you wish, and you do not have to quit your work to do that. You can begin when you have time to move in the direction of the outcome you want and to use your work as a bridge until you replace the income, so that you are not putting yourself in harms way."*

MARCUS: Go a little deeper for us on the mindset required to successfully make this transition.

THEO: *"So, you have a goal that you wish to achieve, you have an inspiration, an imagination of where you wish to use your genius, your energy in expenditure of life, those precious moments of energy expenditure. So, it is to check who inside of you may be stopping you with the resistance on the inner with the belief that you do not deserve to have that dream come true. Know you have a long life to live for that outcome to be, but there are incremental steps to be taken to achieve that goal . . . incremental successes. So, you break it down, for many get confused and think, 'I must do this, and it must be done within a year.' Is that possible? Many things can be done within a year, in two years, in three years, in the direction of the outcome you desire. But dependent upon the larger scale that you might have of that dream, taking those incremental steps are very important so that you are not overwhelmed or disappointed, just as we speak of climbing the Mountain Everest."*

MARCUS: **Speak more to that.**

THEO: *"And that is what we are talking about. The mountain climber that wishes to reach the summit of Everest prepares. Goes to the base camp, the starting point, and then engages in the climb, starts with one foot in front of the other and climbs to a particular altitude and stops so that the body can acclimate, sometimes waits for the weather to clear, but to become acclimated to that particular altitude and once done, and resources are regained, then begins again the ascent to another particular altitude. The goal is still the same, but there are incremental goals set that are achieved by each stop at a different altitude and to acclimate and to gain more resources. That is what your dream is, just as the climb to Mountain Everest. So, give yourself incremental goals as well as the larger goal to reach your summit."*

MARCUS: **What is necessary for shifting our mindset regarding the fear and resistance that people feel in taking the first step?**

THEO: *"Usually what is blocking the movement forward is the resistance. There is a belief that you do not deserve that success. There is someone inside of you that has a belief of 'Who do you think you are?' that comes from the outside. So, we will tell you who you are. You are a magnificent divine being manifesting the life you wish to live. The good opinions of others do not count, for they are seeing your life through the lenses they see their own, and how could you possibly succeed if they could not. So, be mindful of who you share your dream, your inspiration, with."*

MARCUS: **Please speak about philanthropy and the energy of monetary circulation.**

THEO: *"Money has no energy in and of itself. It is just the power that everyone gives it or that your society gives it. It is an exchange of energy, you see, for goods and services. So, if one has an abundance of that resource and wishes to participate and give to a philanthropic expression, whatever it might be, it is not a giving back. For whatever you were wishing to give the money to did not help you* create the money or the resource to give away, so it is just giving, isn't it? And recognize when you give a gift to another how that feels. It is inspiring because you have stepped into that energy of circulation, for what is given one must be open to receive. Receptivity is the key. Because if there is not receptivity in you and someone wants to give to you and you cannot receive it, for whatever belief that is holding you back from doing so, there is no circulation, is there? The heart pumps blood into your body through the arteries, and it is circulating in the body and then it returns. There would not be life without that circulation. It is true in life with resources, with money, and we speak of money because that is the exchange of energy that you use in your world."

MARCUS: Talk about the importance of feeling the feelings of our desire already being manifest.

THEO: "Feelings . . . that is energy in your body. Many confuse feelings with emotions, and they are very closely tied. A feeling is visceral. It is in your energetic field. It is in your nervous system. It is a visceral experience in your physical body which then travels from the nervous system to the brain, and the brain deciphers what it is and how to emote it . . . energy in motion. So, when you visualize the outcome you desire, what is the physical response? What is the visceral feeling that you feel in your nervous system that the body can equate in the brain to make it so to put that vision into the quantum field? For your body is the responder, isn't it? Imagine putting a slice of lemon in your mouth right now. Just envision or experience it. What happens in your body just with that imagination or that vision? Your mouth begins to salivate, doesn't it? You can taste the tartness or feel it in your body. That is what you can do with a vision in your imagination. Your imagination works extremely well, and you can feel the outcome energetically in the nervous system by envisioning it, by imagining it. How does it feel? You have created it. You have succeeded at it. How do you feel about it? What are the visceral sensations? What is the emotion—the energy in motion—from that?

For that is the energy that is fed into the quantum field to bring it to fruition."

MARCUS: How does feeling the feelings impact the quantum field to bring our desires into physical realty?

THEO: "It is energy. Everything is energy. The chair upon where you sit was first a thought, an imagination, before it was a chair, and now you have many iterations of a chair. When someone says chair, each person has a particular picture in their mind of what it looks like."

MARCUS: Earl Nightingale said that "we become that which we think about most of the time."

THEO: "Yes."

MARCUS: So, it is a combination of thinking and feeling the feelings of the outcome.

THEO: "Yes, it is true. That is what is happening in terms of the law of attraction always working for you, always. Many say it is not working. Yes, it is. You have what you have because you think the way you think. You have the resistances that you have because you think you do not deserve them, and that is not a judgment about you. It is a recognition that you are holding beliefs that are keeping you from receiving, and we spoke of receiving in the discussion of circulation, so you are contracting in those thoughts. You are blocking the energy flow, just like if you put a block in your body and the blood could not get back to the heart. It could be death, couldn't it? When blocking the energy to the desired outcomes, the imaginations, the desires, and the implementation of the dreams coming true, those thoughts, those beliefs are like the tourniquet that stops the blood flow."

MARCUS: So, is it just intending to stay on a higher vibrational frequency and being aware of our thoughts and feelings?

THEO: "Yes. Awareness. Intention is the vision. Placing intention and then paying attention. Notice what you are noticing. That informs you. It gives you information and feedback."

CHAPTER TWELVE

END OF LIFE

*"It is not birth to death—for energy is constant; only
form changes. So, you birth into your human body
and when complete with that contract of life in that
form, you birth into your multidimensional being."*

—THEO

IF YOU'RE LIKE US, you may have embarked upon your spiritual path asking one or more of the big questions: Who am I? Why am I here? What happens when I die? The answers to these questions ultimately come from your personal experiences. We love the Sufi saying "that only a fool believes another over their own experience," and it is our intention that THEO's insights will assist you in finding comfort, clarity, and confidence from the awareness gained because of these experiences. This chapter explores the "What happens when we die?" question as we discuss what happens up to, during, and after we experience physical death with some discussion on how to be an effective and compassionate caregiver while still maintaining your sanity. We will also discuss the forever nature of relationships and how to communicate with our deceased friends and family.

An example of how connected we are occurred as my father was making his transition in March of 2015. I was meditating on a Friday morning about 8:15 a.m. in California while my dad was in hospice in Michigan and was sending him my love and communicating with his soul that we would all be okay if he decided to leave us. His body had not been working for him for years, and he had shared with me that he was at peace with where he was going. Two days later, as Sheila and I were making flight reservations for the following day, we received the call from my sister Katie that Dad was gone. I was sad that I was not there. Later that week as the family gathered in Michigan for his memorial, I mentioned to my mom that I wished I had been there when he made his transition. "Well, you were there," she said and shared a story of what happened two days before he died that brought a big smile to my heart. Walking into his room at about 11:15 a.m., the first words my dad spoke to her were "Marcus was just here." This was the precise time I was in meditation, and Dad had been walking in two worlds and had seen me as I was projecting my love to him. It provided even more proof for me that relationships really are forever!

MARCUS: THEO, please clarify for us what you mean when you say that a human incarnation is a journey of birth to birth?

THEO: *"Yes. You all speak of birth and death. Ultimately, there is no death. Energy is constant, only form changes. Understand: your soul births into this human existence into the fetus, into the Earth suit that you have chosen to navigate this planet. And when that time, that lifetime, is complete, the soul's journey, the learning of the soul that it wished to accomplish is also complete. There is a birthing back into your multidimensional energy, the awareness of all that is. So, it is birth to birth, not death, because if you could see yourselves as we see you, we see the energy that you are, the divine essence that is multidimensional. And so, you drop the Earth suit that is no longer necessary and retain that energetic field of the soul that is much larger than your physical body."*

MARCUS: What do you mean when you say "birthing into our multi-dimensionality"?

THEO: *"That means you become aware of that totality of your soul and all the learning therein, that full energy spectrum, the full soul spectrum."*

MARCUS: As we transition into the afterlife, what memories or aspects of our consciousness carry forward into the next experience?

THEO: *"Memories. Love. The vibration of love is constant, and there is the understanding of compassion of the human experience and of emotions. There is a memory of that—an awareness of that."*

MARCUS: When you say that at the time of physical death we birth into an awareness of "all that we are," what does that mean?

THEO: *"That means all of your experiences, whether on Earth or in other dimensions, that there is a vibrational frequency to everything that is a part of the whole. And you will have awareness of that."*

MARCUS: **Why do we not remember who we are when we incarnate?**

THEO: *"You are beginning to remember more than you used to know because the veils between your multidimensional experiences are very thin now, and you have the capability and ability to recognize other experiences, all of those memories, if you would. Many speak in terms of the Akashic records; however, there is not a library somewhere like you find libraries full of books and information. That information is retained in the energetic field of your soul, and it permeates every cell of your body. But it is beyond that because, as we stated, your soul is larger than your physical existence."*

MARCUS: **What happens at the moment of physical death?**

THEO: *"There is a relinquishment of a body that oftentimes is not as vital and working as one would have wished. But there is an exquisite experience of connectivity to Source, God, Force, however you wish to speak of it, the Oneness, the Love that is a continuation that is never-ending. It is quite exquisite. That is beyond your vocabulary or understanding currently. The music, sound, vibrational frequency, is exquisite, with light and color, but most recognize that state of unconditional love."*

MARCUS: **Are our deceased love ones there to greet us?**

THEO: *"Yes. Again, the connectivity of love and the connectivity of soul-to-soul continues. Energy is constant, only form has changed."*

MARCUS: **You use the word "exquisite" often to describe this experience.**

THEO: *"We use it often because that is the only word in your vocabulary that can even come close to the description."*

MARCUS: **How do we overcome our fear of death?**

THEO: *"Don't fear living. It is as simple as that. Most of you resist life out of beliefs that you don't deserve things or visions or inspirations, but when you integrate on that soul level, recognizing that state of unconditional love, it is a state of peace, of calm, and receptivity."*

MARCUS: **How can we assist those who fear death, or is that not our job?**

THEO: "It is theirs to come to, but you can hold an energy field of their acceptance."

MARCUS: **Speak more to "holding an energy field."**

THEO: "Love. That is the energy field."

MARCUS: **When we are in a caregiver situation, how do we best speak about dying?**

THEO: "You only speak about it if they are willing to speak."

MARCUS: **It is mostly about listening, isn't it?**

THEO: "It is mostly listening to what one wishes to speak of. It is nothing that is forced. Because oftentimes, if you begin asking questions and forcing the conversation, what happens is the individual may go into fear, so acute listening is important."

MARCUS: **What is the most important thing for caregivers to know?**

THEO: "It is important to understand, and it is dependent upon what the situation is with the individual, to not force your opinions, not force your thoughts and beliefs upon another. That is true in any situation, isn't it?"

MARCUS: **Yes. What do you see as the biggest mistakes that caregivers make?**

THEO: "If there are memory issues, it would be trying to change their stories, which can make things worse for it will lead to fear and confusion. If an individual is speaking about a memory and it is confused with another one, it is their memory, not yours. You do not have to correct them. Be in their world and not yours."

MARCUS: **What would you say to caregivers regarding the establishment and maintenance of healthy boundaries? We can get so depleted as caregivers that we do not have anything left to give.**

THEO: "You have to pay attention to that. Have a team involved. Ask for assistance."

MARCUS: **What is the best way for reducing stress for caregivers?**

THEO: "What nurtures you? Take a timeout. It is extremely important. You cannot give what you do not have. So, it is important that you replenish the self. It does not take away from the other."

MARCUS: **Talk to us about being in pure presence when we are with loved ones who are making their transition.**

THEO: "It is a gift you give yourself to be present. It is timeless. You are typically so geared into your linear timeframe, this or that or another thing on your mind, but when you are in the presence of one who is transitioning, there is no time. It is precious. So, full presence in the moment-to-moment experience with another is a gift you give yourself."

MARCUS: **It is quite a sacred experience.**

THEO: "It is, yes, just as if you are in the room when there is a birth. You feel the presence of love."

MARCUS: **Is there anything else to share about being the caregiver for one who has memory issues?**

THEO: "Be compassionate. You may tire of answering the same question repeatedly, but do it anyway, with love. 'What would love do?' Understand that the person is not doing something to you, at all. Beings become frustrated because they think the other person is manipulating them or doing something to them. Are they? They are not, so do not take it personally. For the questions that are asked repeatedly, compassion is the answer."

MARCUS: **Many caregivers share with us that they feel very non-supported by other family members.**

THEO: "In some circumstances they are, but in most, they are not asking for assistance. They are putting it all on their shoulders that they are the one that must do, but one can flip that perception. It matters not what anyone else does. It truly does not. What is your intention? Why are you there? Why are you the one? For you made the decision to be a caregiver."

MARCUS: **What if they feel they did not have any other choice?**

THEO: "It is important to ask for your needs to be met, for assistance, and if family members refuse, then that is another issue, isn't it?"

MARCUS: **Right, and that is what I am asking about.**

THEO: "You must call in others to assist you if family members do not."

MARCUS: **How do we forgive our family members for not supporting us?**

THEO: *"Just forgive them. For not only are they not supporting you, they are not supporting your loved one. Again, it is a gift you give yourself. Those are times in energy expenditures that one will not regret."*

MARCUS: **Yet some feel victimized by that.**

THEO: *"Yes, many do when they become tired and then begin to ask the question 'Why me?' Yes?"*

MARCUS: **Right.**

THEO: *"Is it a soul contract? There are many answers to be discovered on the inner."*

MARCUS: **When communication becomes difficult you have recommended that we communicate soul-to-soul. How does that work?**

THEO: *"So, if the ears are not open to hear, talk soul-to-soul. The heart is the center of the soul, so connect heart-to-heart and ask for your needs to be met by another and for their participation, for the heart can hear when the ears cannot. And with the one that is being cared for, you can speak soul-to-soul to them as well and can be informed intuitively because you have the gift of receptivity, an understanding of intuition, of senses beyond your five. Listen and pay attention to that."*

MARCUS: **Please speak about walking in two worlds as we approach transition time. I had an experience at the end of my dad's life where I was in meditation in California, and my mother walked into his room in Michigan at the very same time I was meditating. And he told her, "Marcus was just here." He saw me in his room as I was meditating and loving him at that very time.**

THEO: *"You were projecting your energy field."*

MARCUS: **I did. And isn't it wonderful that we all can do that?**

THEO: *"Yes. Understand this: your soul is much larger than your physical body, so you can project your energy field to other places. Science has proven this. You can prove it to yourself by doing such — transporting yourself in a meditative state or closing the eyes and* breathing deeply and moving in the direction of the place you wish to be and communicating individually to that soul, as you had done."

MARCUS: **Right. It appeared at that time my father was walking in both worlds, one foot in the physical and one in the non-physical.**

THEO: "That is true. When one is beginning to release the physical structure, one becomes aware that you can move in and out of your body. That is what out-of-body experiences are. The soul can do that at will. But in the transitory stages, there is a moving into the other dimensions, as we have said you are a multidimensional being, to witness where you will be going in the change that is occurring. So, there are times when others will meet loved ones and friends that are not embodied and will speak about them. They are there with them. They are in that multidimensional field, and one moves back and forth, until there is the completion of the relinquishment of the physical body."

MARCUS: **It really is remarkable when they are experiencing both dimensions.**

THEO: "It is. Just listen. They are informing you. They are letting you know of their experience. You don't have to do anything about it but listen."

MARCUS: **What do you mean when you say that we are multidimensional beings?**

THEO: "You are not limited just to one dimension. There are 12 dimensions about the Earth. But you are a universal being, you are an eternal being, and you are connected to all that is. You are living and experiencing in the physical body the 5th dimension that is fully in place about this planet now. The 3rd is your physical realty, the 4th is spiritual awareness that there is more, and the 5th is a full recognition of your divine mastery. And that means a recognition of those multidimensional experiences and connectivity."

MARCUS: **I have heard you say that we may even experience the 6th dimension while we are still in physical form.**

THEO: "Yes."

MARCUS: What does that look like?

THEO: "Then you are in tune with all 12 when you are in the 6th dimension. It is just a more refined vibrational frequency."

MARCUS: How does that manifest in our physical world when we access the 6th dimension, or am I getting a little ahead of myself here?

THEO: "Yes, you have no concept of it yet."

MARCUS: Right. So, when we are making our transition, do our spiritual beliefs, or lack thereof, influence the actual process of transitioning?

THEO: "It can. It can make it a little more of a bumpy ride. For an example, one who is an atheist thinking that there is nothing else but this planet, this life, this body, and nothing beyond, are incredibly surprised."

MARCUS: Speak more to that.

THEO: "It does not block them from their full soul's expression, even though it may block their mindset for a time."

MARCUS: How does that express?

THEO: "The brain is part of the physical body, so when it is nonfunctional, then it is not deciding and deciphering the experience."

MARCUS: When you say it is a little bumpy, what does that mean?

THEO: "A push-pull. Resistance."

MARCUS: Because they did not have an expectation of their consciousness surviving death?

THEO: "Yes. But oftentimes, beings call themselves an atheist or a nonbeliever and then come into a crisis, and then they become a believer."

MARCUS: Is it important that we heal our relationships before we make our transition?

THEO: "No."

MARCUS: It is not going to affect the actual experience of transitioning?

THEO: "No, only if you believe that it would."

MARCUS: Speak more to that.

THEO: "It is always good to reconcile, isn't it?"

MARCUS: Sure. We would experience more peace.

THEO: "Yes, but not all have the awareness and capability of doing that."

MARCUS: Same question regarding the topic of forgiveness.

THEO: "It is the same question actually. But forgiveness is a gift, letting go of perceived injustices, and how one can do that is recognizing the gifts and the blessings in those circumstances, rather than holding onto the victimization."

MARCUS: Would it make sense to do a disentanglement exercise before we transition with people whom we have unresolved issues?

THEO: "Disentanglements are excellent for all parties involved. For understand this: in situations and circumstances, such as what you are discussing, there is a relinquishment of personal power, an energetic leak, if you would, of both parties. You have given your power away. The other has given their power away. So, you return it with love, and you take it back with love."

MARCUS: We have experienced a palpable physical release when that happens.

THEO: "Yes."

MARCUS: How do we best "hold State" when our loved ones are in hospice and close to transitioning?

THEO: "It is not your job to do that. It is just prefect presence, isn't it? It is not controlling of anything."

MARCUS: Right, just allowing, being.

THEO: "Yes. Presence."

MARCUS: How do we heal from grief?

THEO: "Don't avoid it. In life, there are necessary losses. There are many times to grieve. You move from elementary school into secondary school. There is a grieving of letting go of that and moving into a new life, into this new way. There is shifting and changing professions or jobs. There are many times that grief is a part of life. It is not only when a loved one leaves the body. But most often, beings avoid *feeling, the feelings, because they are uncomfortable. It feels as if it is an ending and that it would just go away if you did not feel the feelings, but the resistance keeps it constant. Embracing uncomfortable feelings, really feeling them, allows for the ultimate release."*

MARCUS: **The ability to communicate with our deceased loved ones certainly provides healing and hope. Talk to us about that.**

THEO: *"There is that. And having a belief that there is more than just this physical existence also aligns with lessening grief in the knowing that the essence, that energy, that soul, continues to exist."*

MARCUS: **How do we make that contact?**

THEO: *"Ask them. They are not limited to time and space any longer. They are not finite in a physical structure that has those limitations."*

MARCUS: **So, it is basically in the asking, it will be given.**

THEO: *"It is given, yes, but you must be receptive. And understand this: in the asking, do not have an intention of how it is supposed to show up, how the communication will come through, just allow for it to be. Most get stuck in how it should come to them."*

MARCUS: **I am hearing just to allow.**

THEO: *"Allowing is just asking and being open and receptive."*

MARCUS: **Whether they show up in our dream state, or in meditation, or some other way.**

THEO: *"Yes. You use all your senses for receptivity. It may be a smell, a taste, a feeling, a visceral feeling. It may be words spoken in your inner mind, or externally at times, or a vision or a dream or an object."*

MARCUS: **We have experienced much of that, and it is very confirming. As we conclude this discussion THEO, is there anything else you would like to comment on?**

THEO: *"It is not our way to overwhelm but to enlighten the path. Enough has been given for thought in this sitting. God's love unto you."*

There are several important insights in the following session with THEO and Andrea, and in Andrea's sharing of her experience. As we observed earlier in Anne's session with THEO, much healing can occur when you realize that a mother or father who was unloving or abusive was actually doing the best they could with what they knew while they were alive. That they just didn't know any other way of being. We have heard countless numbers of deceased loved ones speaking through THEO share "If I only knew then what I know now, things would have been very different." This awareness brings forth much healing, compassion, and forgiveness. And even though the events of the past don't change, our perception of them can.

It is also very comforting to most to know that our soul's journey is really one of birth-to-birth, not birth-to-death. Andrea has an experience like the story we told in the introduction to this chapter of connecting with her father shortly following his departure from the physical where she hears his whisper, feels his presence, and receives his messages while being overcome with an indescribable feeling of calm, centeredness, and love. Isn't it comforting to know that we and our deceased loved ones survive physical death, and that soul family relationships are forever and live on in each of us?

THEO LIVE WITH ANDREA

ANDREA: You have been teaching us about assisting loved ones that are transitioning. So, my mother, as you know, has Alzheimer's and my sister and I have been carrying the support for her. When is it appropriate for us to step back, even with someone who has Alzheimer's, to allow them to express their desires, because they are still there? They are still holding their bodies. How do we know when they are still capable of making those choices versus us assisting?

THEO: "You have already begun to notice your mother's incapability of that, and she is tired of making decisions. So, what is in the best *interest in her well-being for the time that she has left? Good care and no pain. She is not experiencing pain anyway. So, this is good."*

ANDREA: I have been a bit distant. So, in talking about relationships and boundaries, my mom was very abusive, and so I am often extremely uncomfortable around her. I want to assist, but I am not comfortable being physically close to her so often. I often will tell myself, "Maybe I should do this," and I know you teach us not to do anything out of guilt or obligation—needing to be loved. Can you assist me with this emotion? I have a conflict in emotion with my own well-being and wanting to assist her, with love.

THEO: *"You assist her with love from afar, don't you? You have always financially assisted her. Do what you can do. Yes?"*

ANDREA: Yes. My sister has taken her from Spain. She took her from Venezuela to Spain without my knowledge, now from Spain back to Columbia in a short period of time, also without my knowledge. I feel I need to now address it with my sister. It is time for me to advocate, to step in. I feel compelled to advocate. So, I just need to follow that guidance.

THEO: *"So, talk with her. Do not avoid the conversation. And it is not in blame. 'What can we do together that is in the best interest of the mother's care?' She just did not want to talk to you because you are very powerful, and she is not as powerful, or she thinks not. That is why she is so covert about the things she does. But now is the time that you can discuss it. She learned exactly what you told her."*

ANDREA: Exactly what I told her?

THEO: *"Yes. Now she knows through her own experience, like the child that you tell not to touch the stove because it is hot, but they must touch it anyway to make sure you are right. She had to be sure in her own experience. It leaves the door open for conversation. Not an 'I-told-you-so conversation,' but 'Now that you know these things, let's talk about what would be the right action together.' She will be more receptive to that conversation."*

ANDREA: Yes. It feels to me that the energy of Columbia, where she was born, is a healthy energy for her, extremely comfortable for her, to live the last years that she has there.

THEO: *"It is comfortable for her there. It is familiar. Other places are not familiar. Even if they were in her most recent experience, she does not remember it. What she remembers is the past."*

ANDREA: Yes. It has been very comforting, THEO. If I may ask about the transitioning to the next life. So, my father died many, many years ago, 25 years ago, and I had an experience right as he was dying. I was not there, and I was only 23 years old, and he died very quickly. I remember having this intense grieving that I wanted to get out of my body. I remember vividly in my apartment in Spain that I wanted to jump off the balcony. I felt so much pain, and I fell suddenly. I did not see him, but I felt his soul, his presence, grounding me, almost like, "What are you doing?" he whispered to me, or he said to me, "You need to be strong for your mother and your sister." And a calmness—a beyond this world calmness—came into my body. I calmed down, but I also could not cry. I was very centered. I could not explain it other than he interceded for my well-being and for my family, so I could assist them with their grieving.

THEO: *"That is true. That is correct. And he is watching over your mother."*

ANDREA: That was my next question. Thank you.

THEO: *"Yes, he is, and he was always her advocate, wasn't he? He still is. He said, 'It will all be all right.'"*

ANDREA: I communicate with him all the time, and he lives a lot of life through me. He left so young. I travel the world. This is so beautiful. In a dream, he showed me this flower, the Flower of Paradise, or something it is called. When I travel, I often see this flower in places, like Australia, where it may not be native, and I see it in places that it is not from, and I know it is him.

THEO: *"He is just reminding you."*

ANDREA: That he is there?

THEO: "Yes."

ANDREA: Can he experience life through me? Can people on the other side experience physicality through our experience?

THEO: "It is not necessary for him to experience physicality through you. He already had a body, but he enjoys experiencing with you."

ANDREA: With the energy.

THEO: "Yes."

ANDREA: And is it so for us to be able to heal these relationships where, for instance, my sister and I were not so close in this lifetime when he was alive in physical form, but we got closer as he transitioned? We were able to the mend the relationship.

THEO: "Yes."

ANDREA: That is a possible process?

THEO: "It is, yes."

ANDREA: Does he have a message for me before we conclude this conversation?

THEO: "He says, 'There is only love.' And though your mother could not express it, she felt it. But she did not know how to express it. It was not that she did not want to; she did not know how. She did only what she knew how to do. He saw that in her."

ANDREA: Please tell him that I miss him. And I and my daughters feel him a lot, and my daughters love him so much.

THEO: "There is only love. And it continues. It is eternal."

ANDREA: Thank you, THEO. I am complete.

THEO: "And it is so."

ANDREA SHARES HER STORY

The relationship with my mother has been difficult. She struggled with undiagnosed mental illness that expressed itself in extreme mood swings, anxiety, anger, and abuse towards her children. I love my mother, yet I am extremely uncomfortable being physically around her because of the trauma from the abuse. The first 30 years of my life, I felt like a victim and moved between feelings of adoration and disgust for my mother.

In my mid-thirties I decided to forgive my mother and went on a quest to know about her upbringing. I learned she had a very abusive childhood herself and she did not know any better.

THEO confirmed this realization and taught me that she did not know how to express her love and care for me. I forced myself to talk to her weekly after which I would feel depleted because of the negativity and manipulation. I did it out of guilt and in direct opposition to what I truly needed, which was physical distance.

Through THEO's teachings, I learned that one must not do anything out of guilt, rather, to be true to the self as my duty is to live in alignment with my values and do what is best for my well being. In doing so, I can show up with love to my mother and others in my life. I also learned that there are many ways to express love to my mother and that I could support her from afar as she navigates an Alzheimer's diagnosis. Today, my mom and I are at peace.

Although we don't speak weekly, when we do, we enjoy it. My heart is full of love, and I feel safe, calm, centered, and can better assist her and support her from that place of inner peace.

Once again, THEO's teachings reminded me I can love my mom's soul and dislike her personality choices. As I heal a limiting belief that I had to accept bad behavior because she was my mom and I had a "duty" to have her in my life, I was able to also set healthy boundaries in my relationships with my sister and other family members that exhibit simi-lar manipulative patterns. THEO inspired me to give myself permission to say no to unacceptable behavior and to ask for what I need in these relationships with kindness, while being firm. I live with more peace, feeling empowered as I love myself enough to let go of relationships that do not serve me, even if that is of blood family members, blessing them on their way.

Our hearts are so filled with gratitude to Andrea, Lydia, Ole', Kim, Gail, Miriam, P.K., Legacy, Elad, Anne, Judy, Linda, and Maria for their courage, vulnerability, and love in sharing their stories of transformation. The retelling of their experiences with THEO and sharing of how their lives changed following these interactions were so inspiring to us that we thought they might also be for you. Maybe you saw yourself in one of their stories. Or maybe you have a loved one who has a similar relationship challenge or aspiration expressed in these pages with whom you may want to share THEO's messages of hope and possibility.

We also want to honor thousands of AskTHEO community members who are not named here—you know who you are—who have joined us for various mentoring programs and live and virtual events with THEO that contributed significantly to the questions and topics we explored here with THEO.

It is such a privilege for us to share THEO's transformational teachings with so many wonderful souls who genuinely desire soulfully connected relationships, to make positive changes to live a life they love, to feel incredibly comfortable in their skin, to know that they are worthy of manifesting their dreams and desires and to become so inspired that they wish to assist others to do the same. To be the way showers and changemakers that they came here to be.

And it takes courage to make the decision to change your beliefs to do so!

We also never underestimate the courage required to explore who you really are (many are afraid that if they do they will find out they as bad as the thought they were), to embark on a path of self-discovery, to awaken to the remembrance of how divine and loveable you are, to take the steps necessary to discover and live your passion, and to forge your own uniquely personal spiritual path often without the support of those closest to you.

We also want to acknowledge the thousands of people who have been on a spiritual path for decades who have embraced THEO's soul-based spiritual teachings as they continue to expand vibrationally, desiring to continue manifesting magic and miracles in their lives while being non-attached to the good opinions or approval of others who may not hold the same spiritual beliefs.

Our mission statement at The THEO Group, Inc. is: *We empower people to know and love themselves as the divine spiritual beings that they are.* We hope that this book has assisted you in some way to do just that!

One final message from THEO as we conclude:

"The Art of Relationship is an art, for all things are relational in human life. There's an elegance, an artistry of having relationships of unconditional love. There is within these words an opportunity to implement a new way of thinking, being and communicating. Perfect presence with the self and others is a blessing. That is a life well lived."

—THEO

THEO GLOSSARY

Adult Self—"The empowered and intellectual self. The adult, the mature being, through life experiences."

Archetypes/Personality—"Personality also can be a part of the ego. There are archetypical expressions throughout life. In this personality is how the personality sees . . . Who are you from your life experiences and the expressions shown to the world? How you and others see you."

Archetypes/Soul—"The energy or vibration of the soul in its fuller expression inhabited in a human existence that's expressed in a life most often. Such as the artisan, sage, scholar, warrior, priest, healer. Those are the types, and they express in different ways."

Neutrality—"Unreactive. Non-attachment to outcome, nonjudgment."

Collapsing Time—"Energetic thing that can be done when one recognizes they're the creator. A multidimensional experience. Intend to have time working in your favor. With intention, you intend to be at a certain place at a certain time, then with intention it becomes so as you're moving within your masterhood and paying attention. Many have had the experience of collapsing time. For example, having a small amount of time to get to a place and end up there early. Being on the causal side of time."

Coming home—"Home coming in the context of an orphan, inviting the fragmentation or orphan to come home, to be a part of you, no longer abandoned or set aside."

Connecting with an Orphan—"Identifying, recognizing, being aware of the orphan. Not unconscious to it, knowing it exists."

Core Belief—"A core belief is what starts a repetitive pattern that is limiting. Core belief is a belief about self that has been adopted or has been created that limits oneself from being all they can be. The two main categories of core beliefs are fear and abandonment. There are many sub-topics under fear and abandonment: lack of love, unworthy, and more. Not to be relived, but rather allow one to observe, and to become aware of the experience of it."

Disassociation—"Repetitive pattern or situation where fear arises and fragmentation happens then a disassociation from the event occurs and one fragments not to feel the pain or emotional pain, whatever it may be."

Disentanglement—"Energetic release. Energies that have been taken from one and given to another. It goes two ways. It is a relationship energy. Disentanglement is to disconnect from a pattern, a person, or an event."

Ego—"Ego is necessary for life. That which is the shield to the world. It can set boundaries and barriers between one and another. It is a part of the personality. It is where one can discover how they have set themselves in the world, for the world to see them in a certain way. Ego can be orphan driven. In both the 'see me' or 'don't look at me' experience."

Emotional Body—"The emotions. It has to do with the nervous system, it is an energy field. That's where the emotions reside, very much attached to the nervous system and sensory perception. When you're emotional, you're feeling, and all the senses are alerted. If someone is fearful the intuitive energy is very acute, their listening is acute. Their eyesight at times becomes clearer, hearing acute, the feeling in the body of how to respond."

Fight or Flight—"That is a feeling in the body. It is what occurs in the body as well. It has been the default mechanism for all human beings, all animals, when they feel they're in danger. For humans that can be emotional as well as physical."

First Responder—"The first responder is an orphan that emerges in response to the stimulus in the outer world, or to upset or fear. When one becomes fearful or triggered, activated, the first responder is in the emotional body as a fragmented aspect of the soul. In a threat in some form, it is the response of survival and triggered by fear."

Fragmented Aspects of the Soul—"Aspects of the soul that were disassociated, or set aside, so the higher self could take over in the incident it was experiencing, for survival's sake."

Full Soul Integration—"Coming into the wholeness of your being, being the master that you are. The state of being of unconditional love. The recognition of that."

Future Self—"The higher self, that which you can see into the future of who you wish to be, who you can be, the probability of that expression of your mastery."

Higher Self—"The oversoul, the total soul-self, the sum of all the multidimensional aspects of self. When one lives in that higher self, one becomes fully integrated. It is not a perfect science, there are always situations, circumstances and conditions that occur in life. You become better at living the life when integrated and then having the ability to draw to the self that which one desires and being a conscious creator."

Holding Energy—"Keeping in high thought of the highest vibration of an event, or a person, of being all they can be."

Holding State—"Same as holding the energy. An energetic holding.

Inner Journey—"The inner, meditative process of self-realization or integration. It is the process of it, isn't it? It is experiential."

Integrate—"To become whole. Taking all aspects of the soul into the wholeness of being."

Necessary Losses—"There are necessary losses throughout life whether it is a person, job, friend, home, money—whatever one feels a loss of. There are necessary losses to learn lessons, move forward. Leaving things behind that no longer serve."

Neural Pathways—"The brain functionality where thoughts beliefs dictate how you react to life's situations and circumstances. It is the default fight or flight (fear) for human experience in the brain since humans began on the earth."

Creating New Neural Pathways—"New neural pathways can be laid by the way one thinks. Feeling an experience of positivity can begin to shift that pathway that has been the default into a new pathway. It is how you think. Feelings are the first responder to any condition, so when you're aware of the feeling you can adapt how you think or feel about it."

Orphan—"Terminology we've given the fragmentation, the part of the soul that was disassociated, that was set aside. Stunted in its growth in that moment. Frozen in an event, in time. Could be from your current lifetime or a previous incarnation."

Oversoul—"The higher self."

Pain Body—"That is where you feel pain, in the nervous system. It can be real or imagined. Such as, if one had a limb cut off there can still be pain felt. It is an energy field. When you feel that pain you can relieve it with intention, for whenever there is pain there is an emotional pain as well, a holding on. We encourage you to release it, address it."

Paradigm—"A Belief. It is a belief that is held so tightly that it infiltrates all life."

Present Moment Awareness—"Being present. Being aware in the present. What are you doing? Tasting? Speaking? Hearing? In that very moment.

Sacred Separation—"When separating, acknowledging the God in each one, the sacredness of each soul. Sacred separation is honoring the love of the soul and not bringing into it the history or the dynamics but remembering to honor and love the soul in its pure state. Events, situations and circumstances are only opportunities of growth. Recognizing the gifts of that and taking responsibility for one's own emotional maturity."

Sacred Space—"To honor the God within. Sacred space in the context of that is honoring your own boundaries, that you are a sacred being, a divine being."

Self-Actualization—"Actualizing is action. To act upon. You're actively aware of yourself."

Self-Realization—"Soul Integration. Soul awareness. Connectedness. Awareness . . .to realize to be aware."

String of Pearls—"The string of pearls are those aspects that have fragmented from the soul in the human experience because of situations, circumferences, and conditions that have created untrue beliefs about the self, the feelings of being not enough, or lacking self-worth, and in that they are different ages of the same belief that first was created and then reaffirmed over time with stimulus in the outer world or challenges that then created reactivity that affirmed the belief. So, they are different ages reacting to the same core circumstances."

Soul—"The energy, divine essence you are, the creative force that is eternal."

Soul Age—"The level of emotional maturity based on the number of human incarnations, not the totality of the soul but of the experiences of being on earth in a human body."

Soul-Centered—"To be in the wholeness, the integrated being, aware of all that you are and the acceptance of that. The ultimate self-worth. Loving the self."

Soul Family—"Soul family are those who are on the same vibrational frequency, meaning that they are a match in experience of human experience and are aligned in their thinking of compatible thoughts."

Soul Note—"It is a vibrational frequency that is unique to each and every soul. No one but you has that tone"

Source Energy (God)—"It is energy, isn't it? It is all that is. A solid state of unconditional love."

Trigger—"It is an emotional reaction to what one is feeling, it is an energy brought on by a situation and circumstance, an event."

Vibrational frequency—"Everything has a vibration to it, such as the megahertz present in sound vibration. The solid state of unconditional love has a pure frequency to it. To raise your vibrational frequency leads to better health, better connectivity to knowledge, better connectivity to guidance, you become less dense."

Wholeness—"The wholeness we speak of is in the context of the divine that you are, divinity."

Acknowledgments

Cathy Petersen-Northcutt and Stephanie Pappas for their tireless commitment to sharing THEO's message with the world.

Jeff, Jennifer, Tia, Dennis, Shawn, Taylor, Blake, Alexi, Andrew, Jake, Ryland, Evan, Aiden, and McKenzie for bringing such meaning and joy to our lives.

Cliff Pelloni for his patience and wise guidance in birthing this book into existence.

Ann Markel for making the editing process enjoyable and inspiring.

Ted Blaisdell for his friendship and for always making things sound so pure—the best sound guy on the business!

Terry Torok, Sam Sokol, and Elijah Torok for their love and creative brilliance in bringing this book to life on video and audio.

Stan Lukowitz for his heart, and production genius in assisting in the creation of the video and audio production.

Vernice Reyes for her videography expertise and gently bossy nature.

Rhonda Atkins for her ongoing love and support.

And finally, THEO, our angelic mentors for assisting us in remembering who we are.

ABOUT THE AUTHORS

Channel, pioneer, author and spiritual mentor, Sheila began her work following a near-death experience in 1969 which opened her to various types of psychic phenomenon that led her to become the direct voice channel for twelve archangels known collectively as THEO. With her gifts verified by para psychological researchers and physicists, Sheila & THEO have supported millions of people around the world to connect with deeper awareness and healing and inspired many to expand and explore their own spiritual connections. With Marcus, Sheila & THEO continue to speak, teach, and provide several live and virtual mentoring programs to support the evolution of humanity.

Beginning his spiritual exploration as a teenager, Marcus has been a passionate seeker of truth, shamanic practitioner, inspired by the teachings of indigenous cultures, eastern philosophies, and channeled material. He collaborates with Sheila, THEO, and audiences worldwide, to bring out the depth of THEO's transformational wisdom.

Marcus first met Sheila and THEO by reading Sheila's first book: *The 5th Dimension—Channels to a New Reality*. They went on to marry, found the THEO Group, Inc., co-author *The Soul Truth—A Guide to Inner Peace*, and host the popular Web TV series AskTHEO Live TV.

At the leading edge of human knowledge, THEO provides us guidance for ecstatic living in all areas of our lives and the tools to manifest all our dreams and desires. They also reveal the truth about many of life's greatest mysteries and spiritual inquiries—and the depth of their wisdom is limited only by the curiosity and imagination of the questioner. THEO is here to support everyone looking to better understand who they are and to assist them to recognize and harness the grand power of their own divinity.

> *"We are 12 archangelic beings, speaking in one voice, here to be mentors and teachers. We are guides into this new future, into this time of self-mastery, for humanity is ready now to accept that within themselves. We are here to enlighten, to open beings to the possibilities and the miraculous"*
>
> —THEO

Made in the USA
Las Vegas, NV
01 February 2025

17372640R00134